PRAISE FOR *YOU MUST LIVE*

A light beam of a collection in our dark hours. These poets managed the seemingly impossible: to build life-affirming yet daring linguistic nodes among the rubble of our world and our world's imagination. This is a landmark work, a center from which myriad new ways of thinking and being will flourish.

OCEAN VUONG

Bowing down. In grief and in gratitude.

I feel overwhelmed with respect and thanks for the enormous labors of Tayseer Abu Odeh and Sherah Bloor, as well as Copper Canyon Press, [in] creating this comprehensive gathering of crucial Gazan and West Bank voices, and writing such an eloquent contextual introduction. After years of massive sorrow and staggering dehumanization, this collection represents some of what has been lost—the neighborhoods; the exquisite loving consciousness; the proud and humble society; the triumphant bravery of precious human beings, families like yours and mine, who never stopped speaking and singing. Over here in the United States, we sorrow, we weep, we feel fury at the role our own country has chosen in this disaster, and understand little of what human beings do to one another. But this we can hopefully all understand—the honoring of other people's stories and lives.

Here are their stanzas which served as oars to help them get through the worst days any of us can even imagine. This book should be required reading for every human being, especially those who have contributed to this disaster. It testifies to Gazan beauty and love. And hopefully it will also find the honorable young students worldwide who have taken it upon themselves to advocate for justice and equality and the end of occupation and oppression. This book is a triumph after ongoing catastrophe.

NAOMI SHIHAB NYE

Everyone with any humanity in the face of what is happening in Palestine should read this outstanding collection of poetry. These words emerging from among the ruins of Gaza and from the devastation in the West Bank have an electric immediacy, a burning anger, a sadness over what has been lost, and a graphic sense of time and place which, for some of these poets, is a recording of their last moments of life. It is impossible to read these poems and remain unmoved, impossible not to feel awe for their courage, and impossible not to share their mixed anger and sadness. Like the greatest war poetry, more than any picture, any video, any reportage can, the words of these poets convey the full horror of life under siege. "One day, everyone will have always been against this," Omar El Akkad wrote. Whenever that day comes, this collection will stand as a shining memorial to poets who wrote in unimaginable conditions during the dark time we are living in, when not enough of us were against it to stop it.

RASHID KHALIDI

You Must Live gathers testamentary art miraculously composed, in the midst of genocide, by poets who have borne unspeakable losses, the majority of whom are still within the debris fields of Gaza, survivors now on the precipice of famine, yet with pens in hand, in the ancient tradition of *wuquf 'ala al-atlal,* "standing in the ruins" of the beloved. This is Gaza, as reported by the poets who "sing [war] to sleep" in qasidas and shorter odes, prose poems and meditations, in the sea-rhythms of their forebears, in the hope to "convince the dead they are still alive" among a people "sleeping in tents. / More fragile than clouds." These poems are flares in a terrible darkness, here to show us the way back to our humanity.

CAROLYN FORCHÉ

Is great poetry still possible in the twenty-first century? Open this book and read Khaled Juma's "The Gravedigger," written in Gaza in 2024—and you will have your answer, which is *yes.* This book is filled with poems of utter urgency, poems that give us wisdom, in the midst of devastation, despite devastation: "The children of the al-Bakr family. / I can't find them running in the streets. / I can't find them on Gaza's beach. / Only here they are still running, inside their photograph," writes Yahya Ashour. These poems stun—not just because they speak out of the place that has been bombed-out by the weapons our country has supplied while we watched—but because the voices that rise up in these words are incredibly memorable and talented. So much love in these elegies, so much power. My awe and gratitude especially goes to the translators for these vivid and compelling English versions.

Once upon a time in the mid-twentieth century, Anna Akhmatova thought that poets talk to each other across time and geography, even if they don't know each other's languages. She called this "correspondences in the air." This book is full of such correspondences, the echoing makes history's crimes even more horrific to us, and the poetic gesture even more clarifying.

ILYA KAMINSKY

YOU

MUST

LIVE

Also by Tayseer Abu Odeh

Aza'aat al-Manfa (The consolations of exile: A personal account)

Also by Sherah Bloor

The Gathering (forthcoming from Omnidawn in 2026)

YOU
NEW POETRY
MUST
FROM PALESTINE
LIVE

Translated and Edited by Tayseer Abu Odeh and Sherah Bloor

with Guest Editor Jorie Graham

COPPER CANYON PRESS
PORT TOWNSEND, WASHINGTON

Printed in Canada

Cover design by Phil Kovacevich
Book design by E. Rowan Mena

Grateful acknowledgment is made to the Refaat Alareer Estate for permission to reprint "If I Must Die" on the following spread. Poem text is from Alareer's blog *In Gaza, My Gaza* (November 27, 2011).

Copper Canyon Press is in residence at Fort Worden State Park in Port Townsend, Washington, under the auspices of Centrum. Centrum is a gathering place for artists and creative thinkers from around the world, students of all ages and backgrounds, and audiences seeking extraordinary cultural enrichment.

LIBRARY OF CONGRESS CATALOGING-IN-PUBLICATION DATA
Names: Bloor, Sherah editor | Abu Odeh, Tayseer editor | Graham, Jorie, 1950– editor
Title: You must live : new poetry from Palestine / translated and edited by Tayseer Abu Odeh and Sherah Bloor ; with guest editor Jorie Graham.
Description: Port Townsend, Washington : Copper Canyon Press, 2025. | Parallel text in Arabic and English on facing pages | Summary: "An anthology of poems edited and translated by Sherah Bloor and Tayseer Abu Odeh"— Provided by publisher.
Identifiers: LCCN 2025021577 (print) | LCCN 2025021578 (ebook) | ISBN 9781556597206 paperback | ISBN 9781619323223 epub
Subjects: LCSH: Arabic poetry—Palestine—Translations into English | LCGFT: Poetry
Classification: LCC PJ8190.65.E5 Y68 202 (print) | LCC PJ8190.65.E5 (ebook) | DDC 892.7/170889274—dc23/eng/20250614
LC record available at https://lccn.loc.gov/2025021577
LC ebook record available at https://lccn.loc.gov/2025021578

9 8 7 6 5 4 3 2 FIRST PRINTING

COPPER CANYON PRESS
Post Office Box 271
Port Townsend, Washington 98368
www.coppercanyonpress.org

Acknowledgments

Our gratitude first goes to Jorie Graham, guest editor of this anthology and its earliest, most steadfast advocate. When poetry felt impossible, she encouraged us. And when more and more poems arrived—urgent and abundant—Jorie was our first reader. With acute sensitivity to each voice, Jorie heard their collective call and responded with moral imagination and deep responsibility to the poems, the poets, and to poetry.

Thank you to Copper Canyon Press for welcoming and embracing this project. Along with the entire devoted editorial team, we want to especially thank Michael Wiegers who was so dedicated to this work, so sensitive and thoughtful in his engagement. This was a collective effort. Special thanks to Phil Kovacevich, the cover designer, and to E. Rowan Mena, whose work aligning the Arabic and English text was technically masterful and poetically attuned. With great precision, Sol Kim Bentley proofread the English version, Hala al-Shrouf proofread the Arabic version, and David Caligiuri and Alison Lockhart proofread the whole. We are grateful to everyone who labored on this book with urgency and care, and to our families and friends who supported us throughout.

It is ultimately the poets who made this book possible. Among them, Nasser Rabah, our editorial advisor and friend, played a vital role both logistically and poetically, and we owe him the deepest debt of gratitude. Along with Nasser, Ziad Khaddash and Ghassan Zaqtan helped us to reach out to the anthology's contributors. These poets risked everything to bring us these poems and entrusted them to our care. We were continually humbled by their faith and good-heartedness—by their trust in us, in you, dear reader, and in the importance of this book. We owe them all our deepest gratitude.

Refaat Alareer

If I Must Die

If I must die,
you must live
to tell my story
to sell my things
to buy a piece of cloth
and some strings,
(make it white with a long tail)
so that a child, somewhere in Gaza
while looking heaven in the eye
awaiting his dad who left in a blaze—
and bid no one farewell
not even to his flesh
not even to himself—
sees the kite, my kite you made, flying up above
and thinks for a moment an angel is there
bringing back love
If I must die
let it bring hope
let it be a tale

CONTENTS

Introduction

You Must Live: New Poetry from Palestine features the work of thirty poets from Gaza and four from the West Bank. Most of the poems were written in the last few years by poets living in those territories.

The anthology grew out of a prior collaboration, when in 2021 we worked with the Palestinian poet Mosab Abu Toha to edit and translate a small collection of recent poetry from Gaza for the literary magazine *Peripheries: A Journal of Word, Image, and Sound.* Struck by the quality and originality of the poems, we envisioned translating and editing a book-length collection to introduce those poets and others to a wider English-speaking audience.

Beyond the poets we had worked with then, we reached out to more contributors from Gaza's literary community, and from the West Bank. We were quickly overwhelmed by the volume of submissions. It became clear we would not be able to include all of the many excellent pieces. However, we decided to feature more authors, with fewer poems each, allowing us to represent a wider range of voices.

Access to these literary communities would not have been possible without Nasser Rabah, a central figure of Gaza's literary scene. A mentor and friend to many writers, Nasser manages to hold this community together amid continual displacement and crisis. He connected us with potential contributors and provided guidance throughout.

Of course, it is because of the bravery and genius of the poets that we were able to complete this project—poets undertaking the almost unthinkable challenge of composing poetry in an intolerable situation. And then there were the daunting logistics. Simply getting their poems to us was dangerous. Poems arrived as text messages, screenshots, photographs of handwritten pages, and as social media posts. We tracked edits as the poets fled one so-called "safe" zone for another, finding themselves in overcrowded tent camps, such as in the amusement park that became the subject of Hind Joudeh's poem "Upside Down." Having sent editorial queries for our translations—*Which of Gaza's amusement parks are you in, Hind? Bisan City Tourist Village? Crazy Water Aqua Fun Park? Or Asdaa Entertainment City?*—we waited anxiously to see if a response would arrive. When we consulted Khaled Juma about word choice—*What do you think of replacing the word "loaf" with "flour" or "dough"?*—we were also asking him to find a device, electricity, and an internet connection to simply reply.

What we didn't understand at first is that every time someone's phone connected to a satellite, or received a message, they became a potential target. And to reply might entail life-or-death decisions: standing atop rubble, the signal is sharper but leaves one exposed. And yet the poets almost always replied quickly and with their characteristic goodwill and openness. Each time we received new poems or a response to inquiries about punctuation or diction, we sighed with relief. They were still with us. Khaled, a master baker, replied, with typical accuracy, within minutes: *Hold on, hold on, it should be "loaf." Even before it is baked and risen, it is a "loaf."*

In this collection, we include the widely renowned poem "If I Must Die" by the late Refaat Alareer. This poem stands in for all those poets we failed to reach in time. Their poems—chalked onto collapsed walls, or on the blackboards of schools-turned-shelters-turned-bombsites, traced in sand, or shared in private messages—will never reach us.

Every anthology aspires to be comprehensive, only to be limited by circumstance and editorial shortcomings and necessary decisions. While we expanded our original vision to include more contributors, we decided to feature only those currently living in Gaza and the West Bank, excluding brilliant work that we received from the many Palestinian poets living in exile or as refugees.

But there is ample opportunity to read their work. Most anthologies of Palestinian poetry in English showcase poets living in the diaspora. For example, *Out of Gaza: New Palestinian Poetry* (2024), edited by Atef Alshaer and Alan Morrison for Smokestack Books, features established Palestinian-American poets such as Fady Joudah, Remi Kanazi, Naomi Shihab Nye, Deema Shehabi, and Lena Khalaf Tuffaha. These poets have earned wide readerships. We deeply admire such anthologies and acknowledge the importance of writing from exile—a perspective inextricable from the Palestinian experience, with more than 750,000 Palestinians expelled during the 1948 Nakba and approximately fourteen million living outside Palestine today. We also believe that, regardless of a writer's distance from Palestine or their heritage, they can bear witness to Palestine's ongoing devastation. But, especially now, it is crucial to attend to those whose voices are under threat of elimination.

While we limited contributors to those in Palestine, we made one exception for Yahya Ashour, who would have been in Gaza during this period but instead was participating in the Palestine Writes Literature Festival at the University of Pennsylvania at the end of September 2023; he finished his poetry tour of the United States with a reading in a church in rural Michigan, where he remained, displaced and isolated, waking each morning to try to confirm that his family was still alive. And since we began the anthology, a couple of poets have left Gaza. Hind made it into Egypt, as did Mosab, who then traveled to the United States. Apart from Hind and Mosab, no other Gazan contributor has found a way out of the besieged territory yet.

Despite impossible conditions, the Gaza Strip sustained a vibrant, independent literary arts scene. Readers can glimpse Gaza's cultural infrastructure through the authors' biographical notes: literary festivals, poetry evenings, publishing houses, magazines, writers unions, radio shows, and poetry competitions that award prizes, support new work, arrange mentoring relationships, and select the "cultural personality of the year" (Nasser Atallah was named in 2021).

As all of Gaza's universities have been destroyed, much of this literary infrastructure has also been reduced to ashes. Among the losses are Mosab Abu Toha's Edward Said Public Library and Al-Kalima Publishing House, which was set to release Maher al-Maqousi's fifth poetry collection. Yasir al-Waqqad's personal library of four thousand books was demolished, leaving only a single slim volume intact. And soldiers occupied the private library and writing retreat Nidal al-Faqaawi had on his rooftop before they burned the house down, also destroying his writings.

These poets' careers have been continually obstructed by the occupation, whether they are routinely denied travel passes to receive prizes, or their electronic devices are confiscated or wiped at crossings. Against these odds, most of the contributors to this collection are already award-winning poets, widely admired in Arabic, with impressive literary careers. While we also include a couple of powerful emerging voices, several of the contributors have already reached a global audience from Palestine, having been translated into Bengali, Bulgarian, Danish, Dutch, French, German, Hebrew, Italian, Japanese, Spanish, and Swedish, among other languages. Several have collections available in the United States. For instance, *The Silence That Remains* by Ghassan Zaqtan, who won the Griffin Prize and was twice a finalist for the Neustadt Prize, was also published by Copper Canyon Press, and Nasser Rabah's *Gaza: The Poem Said Its Piece* is out with City Lights.

Some are authors of fiction, autobiography, children's stories, young adult novels, plays, operas, pop songs, television sketches, and literary criticism. They host radio shows, edit literary magazines, and teach creative writing. Some are also journalists, television producers, professors, departmental deans, social workers, geographers, entrepreneurs, economists, anthropologists, engineers, programmers, and agriculturists. They publish in a variety of dialects, forms, and genres. And like all Palestinians, they hold a particularly high proportion of postgraduate degrees, including PhDs.

Many of these contributors are also friends and colleagues in an established literary network. Some poets have collaborated in the past; for example, Othman Hussein and Khaled Juma coauthored a poetry collection, *Rafah: An Alphabet of Distance and Memory*. And the attentive reader may pick up on subtle connections among the poems in this collection—from the West Bank, Tariq al-Arabi writes of another contributor in Gaza:

> Nothing happened, soldiers searched a house in the neighborhood last night.
> And Khaled Shaheen hasn't responded to three messages though he's online.
> I have a few words I must do something with. Bash them out on a keyboard,
> or leave them at the door to welcome kids home, the families that get to return.
> You taught me that.

This community shares their work and engages in scholarly discussions about poetics. On Christmas Day 2024, contributors sent their greetings with a photograph of the inaugural meeting of the Salon of Literary Metaphor, organized by Yazeed, Jabir Sha'ith's son. Despite the immense risk, around sixteen prominent writers and intellectuals gathered in the foyer of one of Gaza's last standing buildings to discuss literary culture and share their work. Among the familiar faces in the photograph is Nasser Rabah, wearing his signature flat cap and professorial coat, presiding over a small table of coffees and a whiteboard.

You Must Live introduces this community of writers, whose contemporaneity and dynamism we wanted to emphasize, to an English-speaking audience. To that end, we made another significant editorial decision to focus mostly on new poetry, composed in the last few years.

Many important anthologies document the history of Palestinian poetry, most recently *The Tent Generations: Palestinian Poems* (2023), edited by Mohammed Sawaie for Banipal Publishing, which spans 1951 to 2014. They introduce Palestine's rich literary traditions to English-speaking audiences and trace the enduring history of the Palestinian catastrophe—a history stretching over seven decades since the Nakba, or, as historians Rashid Khalidi and Nur ad-Din Masalha periodize, over a century (according to Khalidi's *The Hundred Years' War on Palestine: A History of Settler Colonialism and Resistance, 1917–2017* [2020] and Masalha's *Palestine: A Four Thousand Year History* [2020]). It is essential that readers recognize the continuity of recent events with those spanning that long history. To underscore this, we also included a handful of older poems, the oldest being from 2014.

While valuable, historical anthologies alone can unintentionally risk relegating Palestinian poetry to the status of cultural artifacts—conserved but safely distanced from the exigent realities of the present. These poems were written now—giving voice to a living, evolving literary tradition—independent, dynamic, and innovative.

ـ

This collection is also a contribution to global "poetry of witness" composed by poets writing amid twentieth-century atrocities—military occupation, assassination, political persecution, torture, and colonial terrorism. Some of the poets in this collection draw explicitly on that global community:

> I die slowly, oh Yiannis Ritsos,
> Even slower, oh Nazim Hikmet.

So begins Nasser Rabah's "Nothing Kills Me, Nothing," in which he joins a procession of persecuted poets stretching into the past:

> I die slowly, oh Federico García Lorca,
> Even slower, oh Muthaffar al-Nawab.

He addresses each figure as he passes by, suddenly encountering himself among them,

I die slowly, oh Nasser Rabah,
Even slower, oh Pablo Neruda.

Because Gaza is more deadly for journalists than any twentieth-century war, these poets of witness are uniquely called upon to bring the news.

The poetic testimonies in this collection are heartbreaking. We think of Waleed al-Aqqad's elegy for a young friend, set at the boy's funeral and lovingly describing his mutilated body:

We said goodbye
to you in your small death like the death
of sparrows.
We rearranged you.
We placed your severed hand across your chest,
covered your wounds with flowers,
cried as you wanted.

In the poem, Waleed reflects that he has seen so many corpses now, and recognizes each of them, though he has never seen a corpse that is still intact. Waleed's poem also recalls Hind Joudeh's "A Little Foot":

Not a patch of snow.
Though as cold.
No longer runs.
Didn't learn to walk.
Not a rose, that wound.
I breathe it in.
Not a face.
Like a cheek. I kiss it.

As this poetry comes rushing back into our recollections, we always think of Ala'a al-Qatrawi's poem addressed to her children, two daughters and two sons, Yamin, Kinan, Orchida, and Karmil, all under the age of six, and all killed in an air strike on her home, in which Ala'a was also injured. She addresses her children in heaven, offering Orchida her own body parts, as if she could piece the girl's body back into her embrace:

> And give my lungs to her.
> Without them, maybe she suffocated.
> Maybe she couldn't call my name.
> The rubble would have been too heavy for her.

A particularly agonizing plea repeats throughout these poems: that bodily integrity might be conserved, even if in death. Othman Hussein barters with a stray dog not to maul his corpse:

> I go hungry, like you, O loyal one,
> and I don't eat you.

In her meditative prose poem "Gravitation," Maryam Qawwash describes mud slowly settling in a glass of water she must drink to stave off death by dehydration:

> I place the glass before me—watch sludge hemorrhage and leach down—like old history, like an hourglass—we've been waiting for the end—through it, the remains of nations, the remains of bodies pass—they lived once, they had memories—

In memorializing, these poets are also guardians of cultural memory. The rubble that continually amasses throughout this collection of poems evokes Gaza's once-vibrant cityscapes and also recalls ancient Arabic poetry, specifically the pre-Islamic nomadic and Bedouin motif of *wuquf 'ala al-atlal* (meditating upon a ruined abode). In those classical poems, the speaker wanders the desert and encounters the remnants of a camp, and is suddenly struck by physical traces of an irrevocable past, which the poem partially reconstructs into ephemeral, dreamlike reveries.

These ancient poets expressed loss tinged with melancholy's bittersweet nostalgia. But in Palestinian poetry, loss threatens to be sharper, swifter, and final. The Palestinian adaptation of this nomadic motif speaks rather to violent, traumatic losses and the attempted displacement of a people settled for millennia, as Nur ad-Din Masalha documents in *Palestine: A Four Thousand Year History*. In this context, ruins result not from time's gradual erosion but from intentional and sudden destruction. Homes are bombed without warning, crushing their inhabitants so swiftly that, as contributor Maher al-Maqousi told us, they sometimes "didn't even notice it."

Formal elements of poetic craft in Arabic—rhyme, rhythm, and repetition—originally served as mnemonic devices for a strongly oral tradition—a function contemporary Palestinian poets adapt to their urgent task of memorializing what has been lost, if only in poetry's ephemeral images. Poetry's act of memorializing always acknowledges loss by preserving, under loss's shadow, the form of a ruin or remnant. Like their predecessors, these contemporary poets preserve the traces of the past so it might be recovered.

The Arabic word *bayt* means both "poetic line" and "home" (as *stanza* is Italian for "room"). Several poems in the collection rebuild destroyed houses in poetic form, laying the foundations for their future reconstruction. Shuja'a al-Safadi invites his reader,

> let's make up a story,
> let's raise the ceiling of our wishes
> on pillars of imagination.
> Let's make our house—in the corner: a guitar, a vase,
> two chairs. Let's drink coffee.

One contributor, Nema'a Hassan, builds a pub in her poem, which she peoples with a cast of life-affirming characters, including Casanova.

In the context of oppression, even an erotic poem can be charged with political promise, to evoke the American writer and civil rights activist Audre Lorde. And Mahmoud Darwish, in many ways Palestine's most important poet, advised writers not to limit their writing to their political cause, despite its urgency. From his *La Palestine comme métaphore* (1997): "The Palestinian question risks becoming a graveyard for poetry if it stays within the limits of that discourse. If it does not open itself to humanity" (quoted in Patrick Williams's "No Aesthetics Outside My Freedom," *Interventions: International Journal of Postcolonial Studies* 14, no. 1 [2012]: 26). We received poems that were not only documentary and elegiac but also metaphysical, theatrical, surrealist, mythic, pious, and some that are even joyous, such as Kifah al-Ghusin's "Marry Me!"

> Marry me!
> Our kid will restore the house
> Smother the pain of our pilgrimage
> Do a little revolutionary dance
> Over the debris of the colony
> Marry me!

Many poems in the collection are even funny, albeit darkly humorous. For example, one of Khaled Juma's poems stars a gravedigger who dreamed of retiring by the sea but made the grim mistake of choosing Gaza:

> I bought a little digger,
> then an excavator,
> hired all the unemployed.
> Still, it's not enough.
> I have built a business with death.
> Now we are first on the stock exchange.
> Second to none.

Consider, too, Yasir al-Waqqad's ode to his old shoes, which he chances upon for sale in the very refugee camp to which he has been displaced. In another twist on the *wuquf 'ala al-atlal* theme, he caresses and addresses his shoe, reminiscing about their parallel journeys:

> Now I approach them,
> I wipe dust from their old leather,
> from the mountain passes I embroidered
> with my footsteps, and up the stairs,
> and into the poetry auditorium.
> I touch them. There is an ink stain,
> yesterday's alphabet.
>
> I spoke with them like this,
> until the peddler shoved me off.
> I am a story in amber, staggering,
> conscious, drunk,
> here, between the shame of the camp
> and hellfire.

All the poems in this collection are, in one way or another, experimental. None adhere to the classical *qasida* form, rejecting those who dismissed prose poetry and free verse as unpoetic. We chose new poems to study emerging trends. But as with all poetry, these poems are innovative in the way that they work with and against traditions, thereby keeping those traditions alive.

Mahmoud Darwish, Palestine's national poet, is the most important modernist precursor to the present poets. Among the contributors to this collection is Darwish's longtime companion in poetry, Ghassan Zaqtan, whose distinctive work carries forward the modernist tradition. We are honored to include

Ghassan's nine-part sequence "Nine Sons and One Daughter": the poet as a boy seen from nine perspectives perhaps, and in the context of this collection, inevitably also echoing the other youths who have been lost, and who also refract into a multitude—evoking the common Quranic sentiment that each person is a universe, and that to kill one person can be likened to killing everyone. Khaled Juma is also regularly named among the signal figures of Arab modernism, whose surrealist work captures the tragic absurdity of life under occupation.

While modernist techniques and references are evident throughout, their divergent applications result in a richly multifarious collection. Some poems are crystalline, contemplating singular poetic images with loving precision. In these cases, unbearable suffering necessitates the ringing of a clear, pure voice of witness to announce an unambiguous message. At other times, it becomes impossible to coherently speak such suffering that corrupts language. In these cases, poetry gives significance to those linguistic features that remain—tone and rhythm—and attends to silences. Many poems in this collection chart a labyrinthine path through obscure imagery to where metaphors mix, logic turns tortuous, phrasing grows elliptical, shifts become disconcertingly abrupt, voices devolve into polyphony, speakers prove unreliable, and narratives teeter on the brink of disintegration. Resonating with developments in English-language modernism, which also grappled with the consequences of war on language, these poems extend that ancient motif of *wuquf 'ala al-atlal* formally—language also fragments and erodes, its former coherence now only partially accessible through etymological word-traces.

Of those poems in this category, a few comprise excessively lengthy lines, whose meanings grow unstable, and which then fragment on standard portrait pages. To take one example, Othman Hussein's "My Share of Dreams" provides a unique theory of dreams as external material residues that enter the body from without, likened to provisions. This accords with the Quranic view of dreams as gifts from God, also likened to provisions, and the poem confronts the scarcity and uneven distribution of those gifts (rations and inspirations). The poem is also unevenly distributed, consisting of long prose lines that oscillate formally and thematically between dreaming and waking, until the lines start to break in the third stanza when the poem finally commits to dreaming:

> One night I built a dream and moved entirely into it. I decorated it with plains and valleys. I was afraid it would collapse.
>
> Look, my friend, at this insatiable space even universes can't fill. It feeds on reveries stored up in dreamers' reticence.

In dreaming, both speaker and reader find an "insatiable space." In their imaginations, readers now unfurl those first two prose stanzas into single lines, reaching from the margin beyond the page. These insatiably long lines reflect the stated hope of the poem: to reconstruct broken dreams into *bayt* (again, Arabic for both "home" and the "poetic line") and abundant provisions. The speaker tells us that he dreamed he took a ram by the horns and threw it out of the dream, evoking the substitution God offers Abraham (Ibrahim), saving his son. The speaker hopes to find a substitute sacrifice and real sustenance to preserve the next generation from the nightmare of war. He addresses his son:

> Sleep then, dear Nagham, move the world, don't let your dreams drop into the mire of this night's terrors.

As we worked to render these virtuosic Arabic poems for English readers, we made various editorial decisions. We arranged the collection, for instance, in an alphabetical order slightly altered in the interests of flow.

Often translators must betray the letter of a poem in fidelity to its spirit, in a careful balancing act. In this sense, the original and its translation are inescapably two different poems. With each poem, Tayseer first perfected a precise transliteration, made possible by his life-long training in different Arabic dialects, including Bedouin and Classical Arabic, as well as his knowledge of the recent and classical history of Arabic poetry—and local associations. Sherah then studied those transliterations against the Arabic originals. Then the daily sessions of translation began—long conversations between Amman and Boston until the poems emerged in English. When possible, we consulted the poets about divergences and potential changes.

Many of our emendations took the form of considered, if slight, omissions. Arabic poetry is more forgiving than English when it comes to the intentionally excessive use of logical paradoxes, mixed metaphors, and oscillation between concrete image and philosophical abstraction. For this reason, we occasionally had to trim surpluses when we judged that the poets' intended threshold had already been met in English.

Arabic poetry is more open in this regard, because everyday speech already incorporates many poetic techniques, such as allusion, apostrophe, metaphor, repetition, and symbolism. This is a consequence of linguistic and cultural factors. Poetry is sometimes referred to as "the Arab's *divan*"—in the historical sense of a legislative body or court of justice—and is respected as the "collective unconscious" of its people, a repository of cultural, emotional, and spiritual reserves. In this cultural context, poetry is not viewed as a rarefied or elite activity, so everyone, including children, may be expected to recite a little and compose a little, even impromptu.

Arabic also lends itself to the personification so prevalent in these poems, enabled by its gendered grammar. It was a challenge to make this persistent personification sound natural in the English versions, because personification also challenges us to consider a more animist perspective—one in which houses and shoes, the city and land, its vegetation and stones are alive. As such, they too may come to be mourned.

Here, personification intertwines with Palestinians' sense of deep ecology, reflecting their intimate connection to and stewardship of the land. Each species of tree—cactus, cypress, orange, olive, and palm—carries its own environmental, cultural, and religious connotations, serving as an integral part of Palestinian heritage, even honorary members of Palestinian family trees, embodying a shared history and identity. In a poem from Khaled Shaheen,

> The cypress is an old woman dancing at her great-grandson's wedding. The palm tree is a girl waving *where are you headed to in Ramallah?* My home's an orange tree that guards the path through the bare woods.

At times, we found it necessary to highlight symbolic meanings, as in Kifah al-Ghusin's line "Only a myrrh tree for bitterness." But at other times, we trusted that the significance of figures unfamiliar to English-language readers would gradually accrue, until they spoke for themselves—sparrows flitting through the collection, the haunting tones of the reed flute (*ney*), or the horses, standing by as silent sentinels and interspecies judges.

Along with expected translation challenges of grammatical gender and case-based rhyme, we continually noted the relative "coldness" of English. If we did not carefully prepare the English poems, they would quickly transform real pain into spectacles. Sometimes we had to defer the intense emotion of Arabic originals long enough for the English to "thaw."

There is no "right" translation, and each decision entails benefits and drawbacks that must be carefully weighed. Unlike many English translators of Arabic, in most cases we chose to also translate shared religious language and figures into their English equivalents. We decided to render the names of Abrahamic prophets, such as *Yusuf*, into the English (*Joseph*), and to translate *Allah* as *God*. While this approach may mean a loss of familiarity for the English-speaking Muslim reader and the Arabic-speaking Christian reader, it was more faithful to this shared tradition to acknowledge these names as alternative designations for the same referents.

As poetry evidences the expansiveness, adaptability, and variability of traditions—qualities through which they endure—translation nourishes the potential exchanges between traditions. Some of the English translations shed new light on the meanings of the original Arabic poems, motivating their authors to edit the originals. Arabic culture itself tends to celebrate cultural and linguistic diversity as a divine gift; we come to know ourselves through others, and through such encounters, we expand the scope of the imagination.

The title of this book is taken from Refaat Alareer's powerful "If I Must Die." Alareer was a writer and professor of English literature (specializing in John Donne and Shakespeare) and a father of six. At the age of forty-four, he was killed in an air strike, alongside six others of his close family.

If I must die, Refaat says to poets, to their readers, and to poetry, *you must live / to tell my story.*

February 2025

YOU

MUST

LIVE

جواد العقاد

أين أنت يا صديقي

إلى صديقي عماد أبو سيف في الغياب الطارئ والحضور الدائم

أين أنت يا صديقي؟
هل أخذتكَ موجةٌ إلى ضياعها الأول،
أم أخذتكَ الحربُ في رحلةِ الوجع؟
ضعنا في صحاري الذات
طويلاً ضعنا يا عماد،
والأصدقاء رموا قلوبهم في الشمال،
ضحكاتهم، وجوههم، ذاكرتهم

وجاءوا على أسفلتٍ من ضلوع
عبروا الموت
غرسوا أسماءهم في وجع الحقول أهلةً لسماءٍ غابت أقمارها
وغنى الأصدقاء وهم عابرون إلى الموتِ
وأسماؤهم شظايا:
لا تسقطوا الوطنَ في هاويةِ النار
فالحصارُ هو الحصارُ
يخنقُ غزةَ التي أمستْ بلا ذراعين
أطفالها يتامى في شوارعِ الموتِ
يلهو بهم ويأكل أحلامهم الصغيرة
يحولها قنابل تُسيلُ الدموع والدماء
تقلعُ العيون فلا شاهد
الجميع يموت في المذبح الإقليمي
والقلوب تُعلق بين الأرض والسماء
وهي محض ابتهالات. حجارة وذكريات.

غزة، ٢٠٢٤

Jawad al-Aqqad

Where are you, my friend

for Imad Abu Saif, in his abrupt absence and undying presence

Where are you, my friend.
Did a wave take you out to the origin of loss.
Or did war take you on an odyssey, an agony.
We lost our way in the deserts of the self.
We've been lost a long time, Imad.
Meanwhile friends flung their hearts north—
their laughter, faces, recollections—

only to arrive on roads paved with ribs,
crossing over to death.
In fields, they bury their names—crescents
in a sky whose stars have vanished.
Friends still sing as they die,
their names will be body parts.
Do not throw our home into hell—
the siege is still only the siege—
it strangles Gaza, it amputates her arms,
abandons her orphans on death's streets—
like a puppeteer, it plays them, it swallows their small dreams.
It gouges eyes. There are no eyewitnesses.
Everyone is dying in the local slaughterhouse.
So many hearts strung up between Earth and sky—
prayers and stones and memories.

Gaza, 2024

قمر ساخن

جامحةٌ مهرة المعنى المُشتهى
عيناكِ موتٌ وانتحار،
يكتب الندى أزهارَه على وجهكِ
يمحوه نهار الضجر . . .
امرأة من صهيلٍ تعلو في قصيدتي
يغطي شَعرُها عزلةَ سرٍ
في رجفةِ قلبٍ . . .
جامحة أنتِ
تركضين في آخرِ أحلامي
تعودين متعبةً من حنين اللعنة
تنامين في صدري
رئتاي، تفتشان عن عشق الأغاني في شَعركِ
أمرر عينيّ على شفتيكِ
أبايع آخرَ فرحٍ على الضحكِ الكثيف،
أحمل جنازةَ الياسمين
أذوب إذ أقترب من همسكِ.
شفاهكِ تلسع مطري
هل ستأتين الليلة بفستانٍ مبلّلٍ فاتنٍ
يغرق في قارب جسدكِ
تعالي، لا تكترثي بألوان الجهات
تسكنني الحرب منذ أول عمري
وليالي العشق في المدينةِ سوداء
تعالي،
سأهديكِ وردةً انتحر عطرها
وأقبلكِ في العتمة
وحين أضعُ يدي على حرير خصركِ
أتذكر قذيفة هدّدت أطرافي بالبترِ

Hot Moon

This mare of desire is wild.
Her eyes are death and suicide.
Dew-drawn petals lie on her cheek,
washed away by tedium.
Now a woman rises from this poem.
Her hair is veiled in secret solitude.
Her heart is a tremor.
She runs wildly through the very last of my dreams.
She returns tired—a spell of nostalgia
resting in my chest, in my lungs . . .
I search for love songs in your hair.
I pass my eyes over your lips,
pledge allegiance to laughter, to last joys.
But I carry funereal jasmine,
and melt as I approach your whispering.
Your lips sting, my rain.
Will you appear tonight in your sexy dress.
Soaked, sinking back down in the boat of your body.
Come visit me, don't mind the colors on the frontier.
Since I was born there's been a war on.
And nights of love in this city are sullen.
Come closer.
I offer you this rose whose fragrance has committed suicide.
I'll kiss you in the dark.
When I place my hand on your waist,
I remember the shell that almost took my limbs.
Come closer. Look,

تعالي،
خبأتُ ثلاث «مشمشات» من شجرةِ جدتي التي أحرقها الجنود
سآكلها، إن لم تأتِ الليلة؛ لا ثلاجة لديَّ تحفظني من التلف . . .

غزة، ٢٠٢٤

I hid these three apricots from my grandmother's tree.
The one torched by the soldiers.
I have no refrigerator to slow their rotting.
If you do not visit tonight, I will eat them.

Gaza, 2024

وليد العقاد

لم أر جثة مكتملة

لم أر جثّة مكتملة
كل ضحايا الحرب أعرفهم
كل الضحايا
حتى تلك الأصابع أعرف أصحابها.

رأيت جسداً برأس مهشّم
كان منزوع القشرة
كنت أنظر في فتحات صدره
يعبر الهواء بين العظام
كل يوم كانت تسقط من قفصه عظمة
منذ خلق الله الأطراف وجمعها ببعضها
تكونت عندي فكرة
أن الله فنان بارع.

كنا نطمع أن نضمك
لكنك كنت ذائباً في دمك
خشينا أن تختلف ملامح وجهك
أو تفقد ابتسامتك الوحيدة
ابتسامتك التي عرفناك من خلالها
ودعناك في قبر صغير
يشبه قبور العصافير الخدّج
أعدنا ترتيبك
بلطف وضعنا يدك المقطوعة على صدرك
غطينا جروحك بالورود
بكيناك كما تحب
ولم نكتب على شاهدك نازح.

Waleed al-Aqqad

I have never seen a corpse intact

I have never seen a corpse intact
but I recognize each of them,
every one of them, every victim.
Even those fingers, I know whose they are.

I saw a body with its head crushed.
I looked into holes in its chest.
Air passed in between bones.
Every day another rib broke from its cage,
and because God created limbs
and combined them, the idea came to me that
God is a masterful artist.

Still, we wanted to hold you. But you were coming apart
into your own blood.
We were scared your face would be changed,
the smile you were known by
lost. We said goodbye
to you in your small death like the death
of sparrows.
We rearranged you.
We placed your severed hand across your chest,
covered your wounds with flowers,
cried as you wanted.
On your tombstone, we will not chisel "dispossessed."

مات صديقنا الطيّب
مات محبّ الحياة
صاحبنا الذي يكره الحرب
الإنسان الوحيد الذي لا يعرف كيف يقتل ذبابة
مات خائفاً من الموت
لأنه اعتاد الحياة
ترك كل شيء خلفه ومات
كان أكثر ما يخافه
أن ينسى.

دون رأس
حملوه في كفن صغير
رفعوه إلى السماء
كقربان لربّ الحرب
بدوده ولحمه
قدّموه بجسد ناقص
بعظمه المكسّر
وجلده المشوّه
على مائدة مفتوحة
جثة طفل جائع
ينهش العالم من لحمه.

غزة، ٢٠٢٤

Our openhearted little friend has died.
The lover of life has died.
Our friend who hated war,
who didn't know to kill a fruit fly.
He died terrified of death,
he died used to living.
What scared him most
was being forgotten.

Without his head,
we had carried him in a small shroud,
we had raised him to the sky as if
an offering to the lord of war—
worms and meat.
We had laid the reduced body,
its crushed bones, its distorted skin,
on a vacant table.
The corpse of a hungry child.
The world that eats its flesh.

Gaza, 2024

أخطأت حين رحلت

أخطأت حين رَحلت
قلتُ لكَ أكثر من مرة
لا تمت
لكنك عنيد مثل أبيك.
. . .
أنت أناني لا تحب إلا نفسك
كيف هنًا عليك
وتركتنا وحدنا نبكيك.
. . .
أين نجدك الآن
لم تقل إلى أين الطريق
رحلت دون وداع
متخفياً وراء حقيقتك.
. . .
هل أزعجتك ألسنة العصافير الطويلة،
أقطعها لأجلك.
. . .
متى تعود يا صاحب الوجه الطيّب
أين أنتظرك . . . وعند اللقاء هل تحب العناق!
. . .
تقول الشائعات أنك لن تعود
هذه مزحة ثقيلة
تعال لنضحك على كذبتهم
ونعيد للحياة روحها المفقودة.
. . .
سألته أين تحب أن أدفنك
ابتسم ثم قال: في قلبك.

غزة، ٢٠٢٤

You made a mistake. You abandoned us

You made a mistake. You abandoned us.
I told you, more than once,
don't die,
but you are headstrong like your father.
. . .
You're selfish. You love only yourself.
How could you leave us here. How could you stand it.
You left us alone, mourning you.
. . .
How to find you now.
When you went, you didn't say
where the road goes, didn't say goodbye.
You left veiled under your real self.
. . .
Were you troubled by the sparrows' long tongues.
I cut them off for you.
. . .
When will you return, O sweet-faced man,
where shall I wait and when will we meet, and will you want an embrace?
. . .
Rumor is you won't return—
but they've got to be kidding—
let's make fun of their lie,
let's bring life's lost soul back.
. . .
I asked you, where would you like to be buried.
And you said, smiling, "in your heart."

Gaza, 2024

رثاء

كانَ يكذب في حياته كثيراً
كل ابتسامة يبتسمها
تعبّر عن جرحٍ في قلبه
عن خوفه أنه لا يخاف
عن بكاءه أنه لا يبكي مع الليل
عن قلبه أنه لا يحب
كان كاذباً ناجحاً
لم يدرك أصدقاؤه ذلك
إلا عندما مات.

قلبه الكبير
لم يعرف الكراهية
كان ناعماً، حتى على الحزن
بمجرد أن يبتسم
تحدث المعجزات.

لم يرحل، هو فقط غاب طويلاً
لم يقل سلاماً، هو لا يحب الوداع
عندما دفنا جسده، حلقت روحه.

وداع طعمه مر.
يا أيها الموت كن لذيذاً
أو جد منافساً بحجمك الفظيع
يا أيها الموت الرحيم
تعال
وخذ أمانتك.

Eulogy

In your life, you often lied.
Each smile you wore
was a wound in your heart.
You often feared you did not fear enough.
At night, you cried you couldn't cry.
You told me your heart didn't love.
You were a flawless liar.
But we didn't realize that.
Then you died.

Your heart was big.
You didn't know hate.
You were so gentle, even in grief.
You smiled and
miracles took place.

You are not gone, you've just been gone awhile.
You didn't say goodbye. You didn't like farewells.
We buried your body in the earth, your soul flew into the air.

Such a bitter farewell.
Death, be sweet to my friend.
Or pick on a rival as immense as you.
Death, if you have mercy, come then,
take your safekeep.

وحيداً
سرقك الموت على عجل
كنت الوحيد الذي يبتسم
من بين الجموع التي تبكي
أيها المخادع
من علمك الموت بكل هذه البراعة.

غزة، ٢٠٢٤

Death stole you away in a hurry.
You were the only one smiling
in the weeping crowd.
Who taught you to die so skillfully?

Gaza, 2024

طارق العربي

نداء الذئاب

منذ سنوات وأنا أحاول تجاوز الجندي أعلى البرج
منذ سنوات وأنا أحاول الكتابة عن طريق البيت
في الحقيقة أن مفتاح البيت ليس معي
أضعته في الطريق وأنا أكتب قصيدة
عن بيت في الريح لا يصلح للسكن
ولا يصلح حتى لترك نبتة صبّار على الشباك
وفي الحقيقة أيضاً، أسكن الجسر لوحدي.
معي حبيبي، صحيح. لكن نداء الذئاب علي لا يهدأ
معي لغتي، هذا صحيح أيضاً.
لكن ما نفع اللغة وفي فمي صرخة؟
ويا للعنة! في آخر الجسر هناك برج، وعلى البرج جندي،
والجندي يوجه سلاحه لرأسي، وأنا أقف على الجسر
أحدثكم وأنتظر. ماذا أفعل أكثر من ذلك؟
لم يذكر الأسلاف شيئاً عن الهروب
ما حاجتهم إليه؟
ما حاجة الهاربين للحديث عن الهرب؟

الضفة الغربية، ٢٠١٨

Tariq al-Arabi

The Wolf Howling

For years I've tried to get past the soldier in the tower.
For years I've tried to write about the road that leads home.
To be honest, I don't have the key on me just now.
I lost it on the road. I was writing a poem
about a house in a whirlwind, unfit to live in,
even for the cactus on the sill,
and to be honest, I live on a bridge alone.
Okay, with my lover. True. But the wolves' howling is unrelenting.
I have language. That's true too.
But what good is language. My mouth is full of a scream.
Damn, at the end of this bridge is a tower, and a soldier is perched there.
I am standing on the bridge. He's pointing his rifle at my head.
I talk to you and wait. What else can I do?

West Bank, 2018

ظنوا أنه ميت

صورتك على الفيسبوك كانت هدية. لولا الصورة لرجعت لأنام
لكنّني قلت إنّه من الحرام بعد هروبي من العمل أن أضيّع هذا النهار سدى
الزمن وسيلة صامتة للقتل، القلق سمّ صاحبه، الإحباط شيء آخر
سنوات طويلة في حبّ امرأة من طرف واحد أو النوم في وقت غير وقته
لكن اليوم لمّا سألني أحد الزبائن عن رأيي بقصة شعره الجديدة،
الّتي تشبه قصة شعر عبد الحليم حافظ في أيّامه الأخيرة،
فكّرت أنّ هذا هو الإحباط، بعث الموتى والمشي دونما أهداف غير أن تحاكي الآخرين
فكّرت بسرد أشياء أخرى، عن ولد خرج إلى الجامعة ببنطال وقميص جديد
وفي الطريق قرّر أن يُنفقَ خطواته الأولى كلّها ويشتري الورد لبنت ظنّ أنّه يحبّها
وامرأة قطعت بالسيّارة ثلاث مدن من أجل أمسية لشاعر مغمور
ولما وصلت الأمسية كان قد جمع وروده كلّها من أجل صديقتها.
لكنّ صورتك على الفيسبوك وأنت تسندين ظهرك إلى الجدار
بينما أشعل سيجارة سيتقاسمها معي ثلاثة عمّال، أحدهم عاد من الموت
بعد أن أهالوا عليه التراب لأنّ الطبيب المناوب ظنّه ميتاً
جعلتني مسروراً بأنّي أتقاسم هذا الفراغ معك!

الضفة الغربية، ٢٠٢١

They Thought He Was Dead

Your Facebook photo is a gift. Without it, I'd have slept.
I shouldn't waste a day I've skipped from work. It wouldn't be right.
The years kill quietly, panic's a poison, and frustration is something else—
long years of unrequited love or sleeping at the wrong time, in the wrong place.
But this morning, when a customer asked about his new haircut,
which looks like Adbel Halim Hafez's in his last days,
I thought *that's frustration, resurrecting the dead to walk about aimlessly in their image.*
I thought of other episodes: a boy goes off to college in new pants and a new shirt,
decides to spend his first steps carrying flowers to a girl he thought he loved.
A woman drives through three cities to a reading by a mediocre poet.
By evening, he gave all the roses he'd been given to her friend.
But that photo of you, leaning against a wall, while I lit a cigarette,
which was shared by three workers, one who just returned from death
after sand was thrown into his face since the doctor on duty thought he was dead,
made me glad to share this empty space with you.

West Bank, 2021

الزّمان أم المسافة!

لم يحدث شيء، الجنود فتّشوا منزلاً في الحيّ الليلة الماضية،
وخالد شاهين لم يردَّ على ثلاث رسائل حتّى اللحظة، مع أنّه أونلاين!
لديّ كلماتٌ قليلة وعليّ أن أفعل بها شيئاً، أن أدقّها على الكيبورد
أو أن أتركها مثل باب يستقبل الأولاد والعائدين إلى البيوت،
أنت من علّمتني ذلك!
الزمن مرّ ويمرّ كفضيحة، والهزيمة طويلة
مثل صفّ جنود على جانبيّ الطريق يحمي موكب رئيسٍ
لا يريده أحدٌ سوى حاشيته.
يقطع سائق الشاحنة المسافة بين حيفا ونابلس في ثلاث ساعات
بينما لزمني لأجل ذلك دخولُ متاهات الأربعين مع بطاقة الأبوّة،
فهل ما بين المدينتين مسافةٌ أم زمان؟
فلينهض أينشتاين من قبره ليجيبني ويعود إلى نومه.
كيف للزمان أن يظلّ فتيّاً إلى هذا الحدّ!
قبل شهر استشهد طارق إدريس في الحسبة، كان معي في الجامعة قبل عشرين سنة.
مرّة كنت واقفاً على باب كلّيتي وهو يصعد الدرجات الّتي توصل إلى محاضرته
ولمّا رآني لوّح لي من بعيد، ولم أدرِ، أمِن التلويحة أم مِن القنّاص جاءته الرصاصة
ظلّ جارياً فوق إلى آخر الدرجات، عند باب الصفّ، رافعاً يده ويميل نحو الأرض . . .
والجميع ظنوه مات من شهر فقط
فما الّذي يجعل المسافة زماناً، والزمان مسافةً؟
أيضاً ليس هذا ما أريد قوله بالضبط،
كلّ ما في بالي الآن: كيف للزمان المباعدةُ بين المدن القريبة؟
وكيف له إطالة ثلاث ساعات لأربعين سنة؟

الضفة الغربية، ٢٠٢٢

Time or Distance

Nothing happened, soldiers searched a house in the neighborhood last night.
And Khaled Shaheen hasn't responded to three messages though he's online.
I have a few words I must do something with. Bash them out on a keyboard,
or leave them at the door to welcome kids home, the families that get to return.
You taught me that.
Time is bitter. The defeat lasts as long
as soldiers lining both sides of the road to guard the president's motorcade.
Only his entourage wants him.
A truck driver takes three hours to get from Haifa to Nablus.
It took me forty years, driving into a maze. I had kids in that time.
Is there space or time between two cities?
May Einstein rise from his grave to answer me, then go back to sleep.
How does time stay so young?
A month ago, Tariq Idris was martyred in the wholesale market.
Twenty years ago we went to school together.
Once I was standing at the faculty gate, he was climbing the stairs to his lecture.
When he saw me, he waved. Did the bullet come from the wave or
the sniper's gun, but he kept on running upstairs until
the last step, at the door of the theater,
raising his hand, his body leaning toward the ground.
Everyone thinks he's only been dead a month.
What makes space into time, time into space?
But this is not what I want to say exactly,
I just happen to be thinking, how did time separate cities that are so close?
How did three hours of life lengthen to forty years?

West Bank, 2022

بقوّة القدمين

ظلّ إبراهيم يظنّ أنّ ابنه يختبئ في طولكرم
بعد أن أخذ واجب العزاء فيه جاء إلى السوق وأخبر الجميع بذلك،
قال وهو يرفع ثلاث كراتين من البرتقال عن الأرض ويضعها في العربة،
إنّ ابنه يختبئ في طولكرم، وأنّه لم يدفنه كي يصدّق أنّه مات. وفي صباح اليوم الّذي استشهد الولد فيه،
ظلّ بقوّة القدمين يجرّ العربة إلى أعلى، ويقول للجميع أنّ ابنه هناك في طولكرم ولم يمت.
قال إن على قميصه الأبيض ورود قرنفل وأنّه ضاع في الهواء الّذي يتنفّسه وفي هبوب الريح.
والريح تصنع من الأشجار وترابها قمصاناً بيْضاً عليها ورود قرنفل ودماء.
مع أنّه ليس ثمّة قرنفل ولا قمصان بيْضٍ والتراب في العيون، إلّا أنّه ظلّ يردّد أنّه هناك
مع رفاقه بقميص أبيض وعليه ورود قرنفل.
وأنّه سأل أخته عنه هذا الصباح وقالت إنّه هناك، في طولكرم.

الضفة الغربية، ٢٠٢٤

With the Power of Feet

Ibrahim thought his son was hiding in Tulkarem.
After people paid their respects, he went to the market, told everyone about it.
He said, lifting three boxes of oranges off the ground and placing them in a cart,
My son is hiding in Tulkarem, they did not bury him, he is not gone.
Ibrahim kept dragging his cart uphill, telling everyone his son's in Tulkarem.
His white shirt has carnations printed on it.
And he is lost in the air he breathes—it is wind.
The wind weaving white shirts from trees, from sand with carnations, blood.
No carnations, no white shirts, no dust in eyes, but Ibrahim repeating, *My son is in Tulkarem with his friends in their white shirts, carnations on them.*
Just this morning he is asking his son's sister and she is saying,
He is there, Father, in Tulkarem.

West Bank, 2024

حيوانات مسعورة

سنوات من العذاب من أجل أن نكون ملائكة بملابس نظيفة،
وإذ يفارق الواحد عمره الآن يكتشف
أنّ البراءة ليست إلا السنوات الّتي كنّا نصدّق فيها كلّ شيء،
حتّى المرّات الّتي أخبرونا فيها أنّنا لمّا نكبر
سيكون بإمكاننا شراءالأحذية الّتي نريدها وسنكون أحراراً في الذهاب.
الّذي يجرّ العربة يعرف شكلاً آخر للسنوات،
إذ لا تمرّ سنة إلّا وكسرها في التظاهر بأنّه أفضل حالاً ممّا هو عليه.
لكنّي لا أعرف كيف أفسّر لأصدقائي أنّني وبعد كلّ هذه السنوات،
آخذ غضبي معي إلى كلّ مكان، حتّى أنّني صباح اليوم
جعلته يكنس باب الدكان مثل حماريَ الحزين،
وجعلت «أبو الجود» يرفع الصناديق من مكان إلى آخر، ثلاث مرات بلا سبب،
ثم جلست أتحسس بريق عينيه
وهو يبحث عن الشتائم التي يودّ أن يقولها
بصوت (خفيض) اجترح الإيمان من قناع الكفر،
وبحذاء قاوم حجارة الأزقة على مر الزمان حتى صار الفقير إلى الله
صاحب الحذاء، أبو الجود.
مؤخراً صرت أظنّ الجمال قد فارق أنفاسنا منذ غدا سهل المنال
وأنّ المعرفة الكثيرة مثل المعرفة القليلة،
في اللحظة الّتي ننفي فيها البراءة،
نبدأ بالعواء مثل حيوانات مسعورة!

الضفة الغربية، ٢٠٢٤

Rabid Animals

Years of torture only to become angels in clean clothes.
As you pass away, you realize
now innocence is nothing but that time we believed everything.
Even *Grow up and you can*
buy those shoes. Grow up and you're free to go.
The man dragging a cart knows another kind of time.
No year passes that he doesn't break to pretend he's better than he is.
I don't know how to explain this to friends. After all these years,
I carry my rage everywhere. Even this morning
I made it sweep the doorway of the corner store, like a sad donkey.
I made Abu al-Joud lift cartons of grapes from one end of the store to the other,
three times for no reason.
Then I sat to watch his eyes flicker
looking for insults.
But in a low tone he exhorted faith from beneath his mask of disbelief.
With shoes he resisted alleys' pebbles until he was the poor man of God—
the owner of the shoes—Abu al-Joud.
Lately I've come to believe beauty left with our breath
now it's so easy to get—
too much knowledge is too little,
and we deny innocence,
rabid animals, howling.

West Bank, 2024

لا سماء ثانية

يعيش بداخله ولمّا سمح لنفسه بالخروج
قال إن أحداً لن ينتبه إلى لدغته بحرف الراء
وإنه يستطيع طلب الإسبريسو دون أن ينتبه النادل إلى الراء الّتي صارت لاماً
لدغة خفيفة لن ينتبه إليها أحد. هكذا قال.
و لمّا كان يسأل زوجته عن ربطة الخبز لم تكن تنتبه.
ولولا أنه في الصباح تذكّر أنّه قال لصاحبته على الماسنجر أمس
إن هناك طائرة استطلاع في الجوّ ترصد النحلة والشوق داخلها
لما انتبه هو الآخر أنّه رجلٌ يلدغ في حرف الراء.
قال لنفسه إنّه رجلٌ عاديٌّ بماضٍ يخلو من علامات ثورية
حتّى أنه في حياته لم يُلقِ حجراً على دوريّة للجنود
لم يصادق المساجد ولا روّادها، وفي المرّة الوحيدة الّتي أراد فيها أن يكون بطلاً
منعته القنابل المسيلة للدموع عن المضيّ في المظاهرة.

يعيش بداخله، ولمّا سمح لنفسه بالخروج
قال إنّ أحداً لن ينتبه إلى أنّه يرتدي بنطالاً من الكتّان دائماً ويدخّن
ويستطيع أن يمضي إلى يومه وهو متأكّد أنّه لن يُقتل بصاروخ الطائرة
ولولا أنّه ما زال عالقاً في مارثون حرب ما زالت بلا اسمٍ
لبكى هزيمته وقال إنّه مجرّد رجل يعيش بداخله وخرج للتنزّه
مثل رجل يحبّ الحبّ، لا رأيَ له ولا اتجاهاً سياسياً واضحاً
لكنّ طائرة الاستطلاع من فوقه وبأذُنٍ وكاميرا ذكيةٍ
ولا سماءَ ثانية!

الضفة الغربية، ٢٠٢٤

No Second Sky

He lives inside himself, and when he lets himself go out,
he says no one will notice his lisp.
He can order an espresso without the waiter noticing.
Nobody will notice he says.
When he asks his wife about the bread, she doesn't notice.
If it weren't that yesterday, he said to a friend on Messenger:
A hovering drone was filming a bee, the longing in it,
he wouldn't have heard his *r* lallate.
He tells himself he's a common man, no signs of past rebellion.
He's never thrown a stone at a soldier's patrol,
never befriended mosques or their patrons, and only once wanted to be a hero,
but tear gas stopped him joining the demonstration.

He lives inside himself, and when he lets himself go out,
he thinks no one will notice he wears linen pants and smokes,
he can go about thinking no missile will kill him
and if he weren't still stranded in the marathon of a nameless war,
he'd cry defeat, say he's merely a man living inside himself, going out for a stroll,
a man who loves love, has no opinion, no political position,
but the drone is above him with a smart ear and a smart eye,
and there is no second sky.

West Bank, 2024

من وراء السهول والبحار

لدرجة أنّ الواحد ما إن يراك، حتّى يبدأ بسرد حكايات يظنّ أنّه نسيها منذ زمن
وما أن يبدأ في الحديث حتّى تخرج واحدة تلو أخرى، مثل واحد يقرأ من كتاب.
المشكلة، عندي حكايات كثيرة، أكثر من قدرتك على الوقوف لساعات طويلة
أمام لوحة تحكي صرخات الميّتين على أسرّتهم وفي الطرقات.
هل تعرفين أنّ نابلس وفي حروب العثمانيين قدّمت أكثر من مئتي شهيد في يوم واحد!
كانت المعركة على قناة السويس، وكان الإنجليز والعثمانيون يمنعون كلّ شيء حتّى البكاء.
درجة أنّ جدّي من والدي كان يخشى الموت في سهول سيبيريا دون أن يبكيه أحد.
وإنّني في مرّة منذ ثلاثين سنة أو أكثر، سمعته يغنّي باللغة التركيّة لحبيبته الّتي تركها هناك،
في محطّة القطار في الباب (العالي؟). وأنّني أحكي الآن،
مدجّجاً بالعفويّة الّتي يلقيها الجمال في الطرقات وفي العروق،
وفي هذه الوحدة الّتي دفعته إلى الغناء لامرأة تدفعه إلى البكاء من وراء السهول والبحار.
وكان بودّي أن تكون المسافة بيننا أقلّ، أو أن نصدّق أنّه من الممكن أن تكون مثل المسافة
بين الشجرة وأختها في الكروم. إنّ الموت حقيقة هو قدرة اللصوص على إدارة أحلامنا
حتّى لو كنّا أحراراً. لن أستطيع أن أدّعي أنّني ومثل أسلافي، وقعت في الغرام،
وأنّ المسافة الّتي كانت في زمان مختلف هي نفسها الّتي على زماني.
لم أقع في غرامك فعلاً، وأنت لم تقعي في غرام الرجل الّذي يستيقظ كلّ يوم صباحاً
لجزّ عشب الطرقات، ما حدث هو شيء آخر تماماً، يشبه المشي داخل الأيّام
والبحث عن الإله الحقيقيّ القادر على إحداث فارق صغير في اللوحة والأيّام والسنوات
لكنّك تعرفين مثلي، أنّ مَن يغادر هذه اللعبة أوّلاً، ينجو!

الضفة الغربية، ٢٠٢٤

From Beyond the Plains and Seas

Soon as someone sees you, they start telling stories they'd forgotten,
soon as they start talking, one story follows another, as if they're reading from a book.
Trouble is, I have more stories than you could endure
in front of a painting of the dead screaming in their beds, in the streets.
Did you know, during the Ottoman wars, in one day Nablus gave two hundred martyrs?
A battle on the Suez. The English and Turks forbade even crying.
My grandfather feared dying on the Siberian steppes with no one to mourn him.
Then thirty or more years on, I heard him sing in Turkish for the lover he'd left behind
at Topkapı Palace train station. I am telling you now,
with the spontaneity beauty spills into streets, into veins,
this loneliness that drove him to sing to a woman, to cry across plains and seas,
I would've shrunk that distance between us to the distance of one tree to another
in a vineyard. Doubtless, death is only how thieves direct our dreams, even when we're free.
I can't claim I, like my forebears, fell in love. That the distance of that time is identical to mine.
I didn't fall in love with you, you didn't fall in love with a man who gets up each morning
to sweep a sidewalk. No. Something entirely different happened. Something like walking
inside these days,
searching for the true God, who could adjust a small detail in the painting. Who could adjust
the days, the years.
But you know as well as I, whoever leaves this story first survives.

West Bank, 2024

حامد عاشور

القصائد

الحب بلا بوصلة أو جهات
لا أعرفُ كيف يعودُ الناس من الحب، ولا كيف يمضون فيه
مَن يدري!
ربما جاءوهُ محمولينَ على ظهرِ سفينةٍ، وعادوا على متن قطار
خفافاً بلا وزن بلا أسرار بلا شوك في طريقِ عودَتِهم . . .
«من يدري كيف يعود الناس من الحب»،
من يدفعُ الفدية للخاطفِ المهيب، لكي يرفع مسدسهُ عن رأسِ الرهينة وتعودُ هي الأخرى إلى أهلها ونفسها
من يقبض على الحبِ من عنقِه ويطرحهُ أرضاً كما يطرحنا كل ليلةٍ في الفراش، مولعين بالسهرِ والحمى
من يُخرجنا من مزبلةِ الليل-مثل علبٍ صدئة-إلى إعادة التدوير لكي ينتفع بنا الناس
من يقصُّ أثر مجيئنا الى هذه المتاهة، ويُعلِّق نجمةً في سماءِ المفقودين
من يأتِ لنا بأمهاتنا من عتباتِ البيوت-إذا كنا لن نعود-من يدري كيف سنخرج من الحب،
سيراً على الأقدام أم في تابوت.

غزة، ٢٠٢٣

Hamid Ashour

Poems

Love without a compass or direction.
I don't know how people come back from love, or how they go on.
Who knows.
Perhaps they were carried by ship, and returned aboard a train,
light, weightless, secretless, thornless, on their way home . . .
"Who knows how people return from love."

Who pays the ransom to the solemn kidnapper, so that he lowers his pistol from the
hostage's temple, and she's released to her family and herself.
Who grabs love by the throat, throws it down, as it throws us
onto the mattress, each night, crazy for vigil, for fever.
Who collects us from the trashcan of night, rusted cans for the recycling. Who will use us.
Who follows our tracks as we enter this maze, who hangs a star in the sky of the missing,
who, if we can't return, will bring our mothers from the thresholds
of their houses, who knows how we'll exit love.
Will it be on foot, will it be in a shroud?

Gaza, 2023

كلب نازح . . . إنسان مشرّد

دخل الكلب بيتي مع مجموعة من الناس الذين كانوا يهربون من القصف في الليل وأقاموا فيه حتى خروجهم في الصباح، تاركين الكلب بلا اسم أو صاحب .كان يحفظ دخاليج البيت كأنه تربى هنا، يهرب من غرفة النوم إلى أرض الديار، ومن الحديقة الخلفية إلى سطح البيت، متناغماً مع صوت الغارات في محيطنا، يتموضع في المكان الأكثر أماناً قبل أن تفزعه القنابل .ظل صامداً معي ثلاثة أيام من لحظة الاجتياح، تقاسمنا الخوف والنباح والشظايا واللحم المعلب، لا هو كلبي ولا أنا صاحبه، لكننا نعيش معاً المصير نفسه. خرجنا نركض ونقفز برشاقة من بين القذائف، لا نحمل شيئاً غير مفتاح لباب البيت المفتوح دائماً، حفاة القلب والعقل والأقدام شيدنا عريشة من الخِرَق القديمة وبعض البوص وسعف النخيل، نتناوب عليها مثل صديقين، أحدنا ينام ليحلم بالعودة، والآخر يسهر ليحرس الحلم والطريق.

غزة، ٢٠٢٤

Displaced Dog . . . Homeless Human

One night, a dog entered my house with a group of people who were fleeing the bombing. All left the next morning except the nameless dog. As if he had lived his whole life in this house and memorized its interior, he escaped the bedroom for the backyard and the backyard for the roof in rhythm with the surrounding raids. He sat in the safest spot in the house before bombs startled him. He stayed with me from the beginning of the invasion. We shared fear, barking, shrapnel, and canned meat. We shared the same fate, though I am not his owner. We went out sprinting and leaping nimbly among the shells, carrying nothing but the housekey—barefoot, bare-hearted, our minds bare. We made a tent from old rags, reeds, and palm fronds. We shared it like friends. When one of us slept to dream of return, the other guarded the dream and the road.

Gaza, 2024

يحيى عاشور

أدركُ حجم الكارثة

عادةً ما يكونُ هناك أطفالٌ على الشاطىء
يستحمّون بالرمل والماء،
ينسى الكُلُّ أنَّ شاطئنا لا يصلحُ لأشياء كهذه.
وحدي أتذكَّرُ مِلْحَ الحروب،
وأُدركُ حجمَ الكارثة.

كُلَّ مرّةٍ أجدني أُفتِّشُ عن أطفال عائلة بكر،
لمْ أجدهم يركضون في شوارعِ المدينة.
على شاطئ بحر غزة
وحدهم ما زالوا يركضون في تلك الصور.

غزة، ٢٠٢١

Yahya Ashour

The Scale of the Catastrophe

Often you will see them, the children at the beach.
They are bathing in water. They are bathing in sand.
But our seashore is not for this.
I watch them, alone. I recall the salt—
the salt of war, the salt of the Nakba.

And again now I find myself searching for
the children of the al-Bakr family.
I can't find them running in the streets.
I can't find them on Gaza's beach.
Only here they are still running, inside their photograph.

Gaza, 2021

لا عتب عليك

يا ربّ
ولا عليك عتب
أهلي وشعبي
ينامونَ في خِيمٍ
أرقُّ مِن السُحب
أرقُّ من صفحاتِ القدر
صدورهم مكشوفةٌ للقذائف
طعامهم قهرٌ وشرابهم تعب.
أخبرنا
كيف تحتملُ
مدينةٌ محاصرةٌ
كلّ يومٍ مجزرة؟
أخبرنا
ونحنُ يتاماك
كيف نحتملُ عزاءً أزليّاً
لمْ تُصاحبه جنازةٌ واحدةٌ
أو فُسحةُ مقبرة؟

وما الذي يبقى من الأعمار
إذا تشرذمت أيضاً عُمرانها
أشلاءً مطبوخةً بالرماد
رُكاماً مُخضَّباً بالدم؟

سالين، ميشيغان، ٢٠٢٤

No Blame on You

O Lord,
no blame on You.
My family, my people
are sleeping in tents.
More fragile than clouds,
delicate, the pages of destiny.
Their chests exposed to shells.
Their food is oppression, their drink is exhaustion.
Tell us, besieged city,
how do you endure
your massacres daily?
Tell us, your orphans,
how to endure.
Where are our funerals?
Where is the solace,
what happened to our cemeteries?
What remains of life,
when its edifices splinter?
I stir up the ashes.
I stir up the rubble wet with blood.

Saline, Michigan, 2024

ناصر عطا الله

خارج مقبرة العالم

رأسُ غزةَ المفجوجِ بفأس الحطّابين الجدد
يمرر أسماء الأزهارِ المسحوقةِ في حديقة البلدية.
هناك كانَ اللهُ يراقبُ شاباً وصبيةً تواعدا
وكانَ يعلمُ أن الشابَ كذّاب
يراوغُ بفراشةِ شهوةٍ عابرةْ.
غزةُ في الجنوبِ حبلى من زنا القديسين
الذين تركوا صلواتِهم العقيمة تحت الركام
خرجوا بسلالِ الخوفِ إلى البراري الناتئةْ
لا جِماعَ فيها
ولا إغراءَ من قطرةِ نجاةٍ
حفرت ألف بئرٍ عاقرٍ في أجوافِ العِطاشْ
لتشردَ عن مليونِ خيمةٍ
تتفتح ورودُها عن مقهورين
صارت أيامَهم كحلوقِهم الناشفةْ
تتشققُ في مَقتلةِ النداءات
الصماءْ.
طفلةٌ بلا رأسٍ تسألُ
أحبُّ اللهُ الآنَ
وأحبّ أن يجعل لغزة أجنحة كبيرة
ودمُها المسفوك يلبي نداء اللحظة:
يرتبُ أرائك الاستبرق
للمسحوقينَ الذين فشلوا
أن يلبسوا أكفانهم البيضاء
الذين ارتاحوا من نعالٍ شبعتْ من وحلِ الأرضِ.
الله يرتبُ أراجيحَ الضوءِ

Nasser Atallah

Outside the World's Cemetery

The new loggers take an axe to Gaza.
They crack open its skull. God is recording
the names of flowers as they are trampled in
the municipal gardens. He's watching
those two on a date. He knows the young man's lying.
He's dodging the butterfly of their fleeting lust.
Now South Gaza is pregnant. It fooled around
with holy men who left
their futile prayers under the rubble.
Carrying fear-filled baskets, they went out
into the stony wilderness. Is there lust there?
Is there lust in this drop of survival?
I dug a thousand barren wells into the bellies
of the thirsty. I uprooted myself from a hundred tents
that bud for the wretched,
whose days are dry throats, whose days crack
with unanswerable calls.
And then a headless child says—
I love God now. I love
that he gave Gaza giant wings.
Now Gaza's blood spills. Gaza's blood answers
the unanswerable calls.
And God arranges brocaded divans
for the oppressed, for those who
cannot wear their white shrouds,

قربَ نهرٍ صغيرٍ يجري دون أجراس
ولا عقودً قانونيةْ مملة بالمواد المضللة
لمطحونينَ بجنازيرِ الدباباتِ الضخمةْ
قربَ مدرسةٍ قُطّعت أطرافُها من خلاف
وصلبَ رأسُها الأسمنتي
بفعل حبلِ تفجيرٍ ضغط عليه جنديٌ
سِكّير أهدى أرواحَ الأربعينَ محاصراً
لابنته الكسيحةِ في عيدِ ميلادِها المشؤوم.
اللهُ أوعزَ للحورِ العينْ أن يملأنَ
جرارَ النبيذْ للقادمينَ من جباليا
والشجاعية والرمال الغربي
ومن أطرافِ خان يونس وناهدةِ رفح في الجنوب،
أما أنهار اللبن المصفى
مشاعُ المُحطّمةِ قُلوبُهم في المنطقة الوسطى
وغربِ السياجِ المدجج بالمدفعية
وقناصةٍ رؤوسهمْ رؤوسُ العقاربِ الصحراوية
يفتحون أكياسَ التيه
لسيرة الأنبياء المخلصِين.
وهل سوى اللهْ لديه المزيد؟
للمكسورةِ أطرافُهم في غزةَ
بساتينَ عامرةِ من فاكهة وأبّا
حارسةُ كرومِها راهبةٌ من بلادِ الزعفران
جاءها الكوكبُ صاغراً
ركلته وقالت:
الربُّ وحدَه يستحقني
ومعي غزةَ المغدورة
تحملُ قناديَلها المضاءة
لنخرجَ خارجَ هذا العالمْ المعتمْ
سنغلقُ بواباتِ هذا العالمْ

who left their slippers in the mud,
arranges swings made of light
over a little river winding
without the chiming of bells,
arranges the contracts for those bogged
down in their slippery terms,
the contracts for those crushed under tanks' giant tracks,
for those by the school, for those whose right hand and left
foot are now gone, for the head now crucified
on a cord, now detonated by the press of a button.
The soldier, still drunk, dedicates these forty souls he's besieged
to his disabled daughter on her hapless birthday.
And God instructs celestial maidens to fill
vessels with beer for those arriving from Jabalia
and Shuja'iyya and Rimal
and the outskirts of Khan Younis and
Nahida of Rafah in the south.
And as for those rivers flowing pure milk,
they will be given to the brokenhearted in the central territory,
where the western fence is armored with artillery
and scorpion-headed snipers
rifle through the exile-sacks for
the biographies of prophets.
Who but God has such abundance—
for those whose arms and legs were taken—
who but God? For our fruiting orchards,
our cattle-grazing pastures. The vineyard's
custodian is a nun from the lands of saffron.
The planet bows down to her,

لتأكله جرذانُ الهزائمِ
وكلابُ الشهواتِ المسعورة
لتبقى غزةْ حيةُ.
خارج المقبرة
نعم قرب الله الأكبر.

غزة، ٢٠٢٤

obsequious, and she kicks it away saying
The Lord alone is worthy of me.
I come with Gaza, stabbed in the back.
Come, let's lift our lanterns, let's exit
this dark world, let's
shut its gates behind us, let's shut them on
the rats of defeat and
the rabid dogs who devour them.
Let Gaza live
near God.
Let Gaza live
outside the cemetery.

Gaza, 2024

نضال الفقعاوي

الرقم ١١

لطالما كان الله للذين ليس لهم أحد.
الله لي
أما أنتم، فصلّوا عليّ ولا تطيلوا
الجثث المجهولة تستأنس بالوحشة،
ادفنوني كجثة مجهولة
وبدل اسمي
ضعوا رقماً غامضاً.
انحتوا خطين عموديين وقولوا:
يوماً ما
من هذا التراب ستنبعث جثة مطبوعة بالرقم ١١
رقمي المفضل في كرة القدم.
أنا أعرف نفسي-صدقوني-
أنا ثور أهوج
قضيت عمري أركض خلف كرة
ولا أظنني سأتوقف.
ربما
لديّ سبعون سنة كاملة
آكل وأشرب وأصمت وأضحك وألعب وأقرأ وأحزن وأنام.
ربما تبقى نصفها
ربما لا،
إلا أنني أهرع كالممسوس إلى غرفتي
أتلوّى على الأرض كمن لا يطيق الانتظار
كمن ليس لديه وقت
كمن يريد أن يقول شيئاً مهماً
قبل أن يموت.

غزة، ٢٠٢٢

Nidal al-Faqaawi

The Number 11

God is for me.
God has always been for those who have no one.
As for you, pray for me but make it brief.
Anonymous corpses find solace in their loneliness.
Bury me as a nameless corpse.
Use a number
instead of my name.
Engrave two vertical lines and say—
someday, from this sand, will emerge corpse number 11.
It's my favorite football number.
I know myself—believe me—
I'm a bull.
I spent my life running after a ball.
I don't think I'll stop.
Even if
I have seventy years left
to eat, drink, break the monotony, stay silent, laugh, play, read, grieve, then sleep.
Even if I get just half of that.
Which is not likely.
Therefore I rush like a man beaten by a devil into my room,
I writhe on the floor, I can't wait,
I don't have any time left,
I want to feel something important
before I die.

Gaza, 2022

أنيس غنيمة

أقل من أن يعجب أحداً

عندي غرفة مؤخراً
منذ ١٩٤٨ لم يدخلها هواء
لذا حوّلتها إلى مسرح
كل ليلةٍ ألقي من خشبته قصيدة على جمهورٍ غائب
سعيداً بموسيقى الآلام التي تعزف
دون أن يسمعها أحد.

وعندي وردةٌ
أعتقد أنها ستموت قريباً
أكتب فقط كي أعبر لها عن إعجابي
ولدّي كلب
اشتريته بكل ما أملك من أصدقاء
كل ليلة أذهب في نزهة مع غراب ضائع
وأحتفظ بدرّاجة
سرقتها من طفل
كل نهار أقطع ٤٥ كيلومتراً
دون أن أنتبه . . .

مع هذا كلّه
أعرف أني وحيدٌ وغريبٌ هنا
حلمي أن أقابل امرأة على الدرج
هناك سأهديها قصيدتي هذه
وأعرف تماماً-منذ الآن-
أنها لن تعجبها.

غزة، ٢٠١٦

Anes Ganema

Too Little

I recently got a room.
No air has entered it since 1948.
So I turned it into a theater.
From its stage, I recite poetry each night to an absent audience.
They're thrilled with the pained music that plays,
that nobody hears.

I have a flower.
I think it will wither soon.
I only write to praise it.
And I have a dog
that I bought with all my friends.
Each night we go for a stroll. Joined by a lost crow.
And I keep a bicycle
I stole from a child that
I ride 45 kilometers daily
without noticing.

Despite this,
I know I am a stranger.
I dream of meeting someone by the stairs,
of giving her this poem.
I know already
it is not enough.

Gaza, 2016

الندوب وحدها

من خشبٍ
لا يصلح للدفنِ
بنى ميتون غرفتي
إنني محاصرٌ على الدوام
بقبورٍ لا أفلحُ بسقايتها.

أصيصُ الوردة التي بلا اسمٍ،
فيه طينٌ، لا معنىً له،
منه خلقتُ، أنا المبتلّ
حتى أخمص جذوري
بالماء
المتجدد.

شيئاً فشيئاً تموت الشجرة
الندوب وحدها تقاوم الفأس.

غزة، ٢٠١٧

My Roots

From wood
unfit for coffins,
the dead built my room.
I am walled in
by graves. I forget to water them.

The pot of the nameless flower
is made from clay
from which I was also molded. Meaningless. Soaked
down to my roots
with waters that are ever renewed.

Little by little, the tree dies.
Only its scars resist the axe.

Gaza, 2017

صلاة يومية لوردة الشرفة

طوال حياتي بلا أحد،
أحفر بالطوبِ وجنتيّ
اللتين مثل قبرٍ منبوش
أرسمُ بيتي قبالة نهرٍ
بلا ماءٍ

لأعطشَ لك أيها العالم البغيضُ
أيها الأصدقاء البعيدون والتائهون
أيتها الربّاتُ
يا صفوة ما في العدم.

أعبد وردة
وأقدّس عيني البلاستيك
لا أعجبُ أحداً
كل قطارٍ يمضي
أصفّق له بيدينِ من فولاذٍ
مرتاحاً على سكّةٍ لا تقود لشيء.

غزة، ٢٠١٧

Daily Prayer for the Terrace Rose

All my life I've been alone.
With bricks I dig.
My cheeks gaunt like raised graves.
I sketch my house
by the dry riverbed.

I thirst for you, loathsome world,
distant and lost friends,
goddesses,
gentlefolk of nothingness.

I worship a rose.
I sanctify my plastic eyes.
I impress no one.
Every train that goes by
I applaud.
On this track, I am fine. It goes nowhere.
I am fine on this track to nowhere.
I applaud with hands of steel.

Gaza, 2017

حيدر الغزالي

إن كان قدري الجنة

أريدُ ألّا يكون كل شيء سهلاً
تلكَ أيادٍ خلقت للحب
وللصخور أيضاً.
إن كان قدري الجنّة، ستكون طلباتي غريبة
وأنا أبني بيتي الأوّل
غرفةَ أطفالي
وحديقةَ المنزل
وأريدُ لكل حجرٍ أنام تحته قصة وجع
يا لها من راحة.

سأعيدُ الفيلم كلّه
-وأنا في الجنة-أرقص لأنّ باباً مشرقاً سيُفتح
نعم، أريدُ أن أُحبطَ حيال ذلك.
وأكبرُ بين حمقى يتسمّرون في وجهي
جيّدٌ أن أسقطَ في بعضها
بينما الكلّ غارقٌ في النعيم
سأكون قد سقطتُ في فخاخ الحمقى
وتخرجت من جامعةٍ أحبها
وبنيتُ من المشقة
بيتاً مليئاً بالنوافذ والصغار
وأقطر حينها عرقاً:
أوه، لقد أنجزت المهمة
لقد عشت الحياة.

غزة، ٢٠٢٤

Haider al-Ghazali

Had my fate been heaven, my wishes would've been bizarre

I don't want everything to be easy.

These hands are my heart. They are for stones.
They will build my first house.
A room for children. An orchard.
The stone I sleep beneath is a terrible story.

Let me rewind the entire film to the start—

I'm in heaven—dancing before a beaming gate. It will open.
Yes, I want to go down again.

I grow up among fools who stare at my face.
It is okay to fall in with them.
While everyone is busy with bliss
I fall into their traps.

Then I graduate from my favorite university.
I work hard. I build my house.
I put in windows. I fill them with little ones.
Here I am now, do you see me dripping with
sweat:
Oh, I've done it, I say again,
I've lived a life.

Gaza, 2024

على الحربِ أن تنتظر

أن تأخذ إجازةً
ريثما ألتقي بحبيبتي
ويصير لدينا قصة حب، وعائلة
وأطفالاً يجعلون ليديّ
وظيفةً أخرى غير الارتجاف.
ويصير لاسمي لقب «بابا»
ولثغة في حروفه.

سأقلّم أظافرك أيتها الحرب
سأغسلُ يديكِ من لحمِ أمتي
إن شئتِ
وأغني إليكِ أغنية لكي تنامي
شرطَ أن يكبر أبنائي
مع أولادهم
يضعون ورداً فوق قبري
لقلبٍ جرّب الحياة
وصار عليه أن يموت.

غزة، ٢٠٢٤

The War Must Wait

until I take a vacation
take on the part written
for me—about love, about family.
Children to occupy my hands
so they will stop shaking,
to change my name to Papa
with a lisp.

Dear war, I will trim your fingernails,
I will wash your hands
of my people's flesh.
I will sing you to sleep.
Just let my children
grow and have children
who will put flowers on the grave
of this heart who tried life
and must now die.

Gaza, 2024

أيتها الإبادة

خذي شكلي
وأمنياتي
ارتدي ملابسي
خذي أقدامي المسطحة
ومشيتي العرجاء
عيشي تجاربَ حبي
وخجلي
صادقي رفاقاً
لا يملكون أعماراً كافية
تعلقي بهم كثيراً.
استيقظي باكراً مثلي
تغسلين وجهكِ بالضوء
تروين ظمأ النعناع
وتحلمين.
دون أن تدري
أنّ موتَ النائمين أسهل.

خذي حياتي
علّكِ تموتين.

غزة، ٢٠٢٤

O Annihilation

take my shape
take my hopes
wear my clothes
take my flat feet
my limping gait
live my love stories for me
take my meekness
make my friends
whose lives aren't long enough
and cling to them.
Wake up early like me
wash your face in light
you who can still dream.
You can never die
in your sleep.

Gaza, 2024

علاء الغول

دخان وعناق

لا تكترثْ
ستظل هذي الحربُ غائرةً
كجرحٍ واسعٍ في الذاكرةْ.
لن تنتهي من دفتري وأنا سأكتبُ
دائماً عن رغوةِ البحرِ التي أضحتْ
كما لونُ الدقيقِ كما أرى كبريتُ
مقذوفاتِ ما قبلَ الظهيرةِ فوق
أسطحنا وفي الساحاتِ تملؤها دخاناً
أو غباراً. هل ترين سماءنا كيف استحالت
خيمةً مفتوحةً للبردِ؟ هذا يا حبيبتي
البعيدةَ ليس مما كان في صورِ الخيالِ
عن المكان، لقد تمنينا معاً تغييرَ ألوانِ
الطريقِ، أنا أحبكِ حاملاً شوقي وأسمائي
وما في رغبتي من أمنياتٍ لا أراها الآن
هادئةً تناسبني، وأما الحبُّ فالدنيا
تؤمِّنُ لي بقايا من عناقٍ كان يمكن
أن يكونَ لنا هدوءاً من صباحٍ واسعٍ.

غزة، ٢٠٢٣

Ala'a al-Ghoul

Smoke and Embrace

Never mind,
this war will continue
deep in the memory like a wound.
It doesn't end in my notebook. I keep writing
about sea-foam that blows in
flour-colored as sulfur shells
just before noon. They pass
over our rooftops. They fill
city squares with their smoke
and dust. Do you see that sky.
Do you see our tent open to the cold.

This, my distant one, my beloved,
was not in our vision
of the place. We wanted to change
the street colors, remember. I love you. I cradle
my nostalgia, my names, these wishes—
I can't see you right now. It is so
quiet for me here. It is suitable. I hold the ghost
of your embrace. This could have been
the calm of a vast morning.

Gaza, 2023

المزمور الحادي والخمسون بعد المائتين (غواية قديمة)

عصافيري القديمةُ لا تزالُ تزورني
يا أيها الدوريُّ حرِّرْني بشدوكَ مثلما
أطلَقتَ هذا الصبحَ من جفنيكَ من أحضانِ
تلكَ الشمسِ صوتُكَ غرفتي الملأى برائحةِ
الشروقِ ورغبةِ الدنيا الجميلةِ في اختياري

مرةً أخرى لأعبرها بروحي والتفاؤلِ إنني طفلُ
الحقيقةِ حاملُ النورِ الخفيِّ أُضيءُ طرقاتي
بنفسي يا عصافيري البريئةَ كيف حالُ الوردِ
خلفَ السورِ بين بيوتِنا الأولى وفي أشلائها
وخرائبِ الذكرى وهذي الحربِ؟

خبرني عن الدراقِ والماضي ولونِ
اللوزِ يا نيسانُ يا فرحَ السماءِ وقصَّتي
مع كلِّ ما هو صادقٌ في العُمْرِ
هل ستظلُّ أوفى لي وتبعثُ فيَّ آمالي
العظامَ كما فعلتَ على ضفافِ الحلمِ؟ خذْني
من يدي لأمرَّ من نفقِ التساؤلِ لليقينِ
ومن جمودِ الفكرِ للتحليقِ في ما ليسَ مُجْتَرّاً

وقوِّيني برائحةِ القرنفلِ فهي ذاكرةٌ بحجمِ
خرافةٍ لا تستطيعُ الموتَ
نافذتي انتظارٌ فرصةٌ أخرى لألحقَ
بالطيورِ وغربةٌ طوعيةٌ في الوعي في
تبريرِ خطواتي إلى الدنيا الجريئةِ
كيف لا والقلبُ نَبْضُ الحبِّ عن قصدٍ
ولحظاتُ الندى والأغنياتُ.

غزة، ٢٠٢٤

Psalm 251: An Ancient Temptation

My old sparrows still visit me.
Sparrows, free me with your song, I say,
as you released this morning from your eyelids.
Your song is my room—
filling with the aroma of dawn now,
and the stunning love of this world that chooses me.

Once again crossing life with my soul and my hope. I am a child,
a hidden bearer of light,
illuminating my path by myself for myself.
O innocent birds, how are the roses
beyond that wall? The wall that stands between our first homes and their remains.

Remind me about the peaches—the feel, the color.
About almonds. About Aprils. Also the joy of the sky. Also my story.
Tell me about all that was true in this life.
Will you be faithful? Will you resurrect my hopes?
As you did on the banks of that dream? Take me
by the hand. Let's pass through a runnel of doubts,
of certitudes. Through stagnation into the new.

Fortify me with the scent of carnations.
Fortify me with a myth that won't die.
Please vindicate my steps into the bold world
where the heart pulses with love on purpose,
remind me of those moments of dew and song.
I wait at my window to catch up with you.

Gaza, 2024

كفاح الغصين

تزوجني

لننجبَ فارساً أسمر
يشقُ غبارَ نكبتنا
يعيدُ جوادَ هيبتنا
بأرضِ الزيتِ والزعتر
فإن العقمَ ملءُ الكون
وعلمي ضاعَ مِنْهُ اللون
ومثلي من ذواتِ الصون
ومهري خاتمٌ أصغر.
تزوجني
لننجبَ من يعيد الدار
ويخرسُ غصةَ المشوار
ويرقصُ رقصةَ الثوار
على أشلاءِ مستعمر.
تزوجني
ولا شيء نظيفٌ يشهدُ القدّاس
لا الجدران
ولا الحراس
ولا الحكام
ولا العسكر.

فشاهدُ عرسنا الأوحد
هو وطني
يزيننا بعقد الفلِ والريحانِ والعنبر
ويُطربنا بموال العتابا من شفاه الموتِ
وينثرُ فوقنا الوروار والدوري.

Kifah al-Ghusin

Marry Me!

Marry me!
Marry me!
We'll have a dark knight
Revive the glory of our horse
In the land of oil and thyme
All the universe is barren
And my flag flies colorless
I am a chaste woman
My dowry's just a little ring
Marry me!
Our kid will restore the house
Smother the pain of our pilgrimage
Do a little revolutionary dance
Over the debris of the colony
Marry me!
Nothing is clean in the sanctuary:
Not the walls
Not the guards
Not the rulers
Not the soldiers.

The only witness to our wedding
Is my homeland.
It adorns us in jasmine, in basil, and amber bracelets.
It serenades us with the folk songs of *ataaba* from death's own lips,

تزوجني
لننجبَ من يردُّ القدس
ويقهرُ كبرياءَ الفرس
ويهدي حرفهُ للخرس
ويمسحُ دمعةَ الأزهر
تزوجني.

غزة، ٢٠١٥

Sprinkled down by bee-eaters all over our heads.
Marry me!
Our children will restore Jerusalem,
Dedicate our alphabet to the mute,
Wipe the tears from al-Azhar—
Oh, marry me.

Gaza, 2015

خذني إلى بوابات المدينة

خذيني حيث رائحتي ببابِ الحي
صغاراً وقتها كنّا
ونعدو علّنا نكبُر
نُصلّي علّنا نكبُر
ونلبسُ كومةَ الأثوابِ من دولاب جدتنا
نظَنُّ بأننا نكبُر
وأذكرُ كيف كان السيلُ يرعبنُا
وصوتُ الطبلةِ السحريِّ في حاراتنا
أذكُر.
وكنا نرفعُ الكفين نحو الله
كي تمضي طفولتنا بغمضةِ عينْ
نتمتمُ علّنا نكبُر
وكنا نمزجُ الأيام بالسُكَّر
نوزعُ كعكبانَ الحُّبِ إذ نسمُر
ونحشو الوقتَ بالأحلامِ
فتحشونا لكي تَعْبُر
وتوهمُنا بأن الوردَ يجثو كي يراقصَنا
على الأبوابِ إذ نكبُر.
وأسرعت السنونُ الخضر
وحين فتحتُ أبوابي
فلا وردٌ لقيت ولا ندى
إلاه شجرُ المُر
تكاثر في مداراتي
يقهقهُ من سذاجتنا
ولهفتنا لكي نكبُر.

Take me to the city gates

Take me to the city gates
Where my perfume still lurks.
Take me to when we were little,
Running so we could come of age.
We prayed we'd grow up.
We put on piles of dresses from Grandma's closet
Thinking we were growing up.
Recall that flash flood. How it terrified us.
And the magic drumming in the alleys.
I still remember.
We raised our palms to God
To make childhood pass in a blink.
We mumbled, *Maybe we'll grow up.*
We mixed our days with sugar,
Shared love candies, chitchatting into the night.
We stuffed time with dreams,
Stuffed ourselves so we could get through it.
We fancied long-stemmed roses bowed
At the door to waltz us into adulthood.
The green years rushed by fast.
When I flung open my front door,
I found no dew-sprinkled flowers.
Only a myrrh tree for bitterness
That germinated in my presence.
And the green years rushed by fast.

وأسرعت السنون الخُضر
وما زالت عباءاتي تفتش عنكِ رائحتي
بباب الحي . . .
وتصرخ ليتنا يا دار لم نكبُر.

غزة، ٢٠١٩

My dresses, my perfume, they still search
For you by the city gates, crying
If only we hadn't grown up. Oh home.
And the green years rush by fast.

Gaza, 2019

نعمة حسن

لنصنع غيمة

أين يذهب صوت فيروز حين تنقطع أسلاك الكهرباء؟
تشعل عود ثقاب ليراها الليل
الشموع بقيت في البيوت المهاجرة
وسطح الجيران يجلس وحيداً.

هل هناك معبر آمن؟
العارفون بالطرق يحملون قنديلاً
عناوين البلاد ثابتة.

أنا امرأة من المدينة التي لا تغفو
أدخن كثيراً
حتى لا يراني غبار الحرب.

كغريقٍ ينجو من فعلته . . .
يستعيد رئتيه الهاربتين نحو الموج
يلزم الملح بالحياد
أحاول طهو الطعام
تقليم أظافري
الاعتناء بالسلحفاة الوحيدة في زاوية بيتي
ووضع القليل من عطر المساء
في وقت آخر
أذهب لسماع صوت الطائرات
الحديث مع جارتي عن موعد الكهرباء
مشاهدة الأغنيات بدل نشرة الأخبار
إقناع الموتى أنهم ما زالوا أحياء

Nema'a Hassan

To Create a Cloud

Where does Fairuz's voice go in a power outage?
She strikes a match so the night can see her face.
The candle still stands in the abandoned home
as the neighbor's roof lies down.

Is there safe passage?
Those who know these roads carry lanterns—
our country's addresses last forever.

I am a woman from this city that never falls
asleep. I smoke too much
so I can't be seen in the dust of war.

Like a drowning person who survives,
I recover the lungs
I'd surrendered to waves.
Oh salt. I'm trying to cook now.
I've cut my nails.
I'm taking care of a lonely turtle that squats in the corner of my room.

I go to hear the warplanes.
I go talk to my neighbor about the power.
When will it be restored?
I watch music videos instead of news.
I convince the dead they are still alive.

وترتيب خزانتي قبل المغادرة.
اليوم
المدينة تحلق
والجميع يرقص على الحافة
لن ينجو إلا من تذوق رائحة الرصاص
لا أملك منطاداً
سأشرب قهوتي قبل نفاذ البن من الدكان
وأدّعي أنني بخير.

الكثير من الأيدي المبتورة تحاول مصافحتي
ركوة القهوة تهتز على النار
والعزاءات لا تنتظر
هل استبدل المطر وجهته
يتساءل حفار القبور.

كم ليمونة على الشجرة؟
يخيفني قلق العصافير
وحموضة المواسم
وبكاء طفل شعره (كيرلي)
لم يعد لأمه بعد أن أغلقت أبواب الكنائس.

لدي الكثير من الحب في قلبي
استهلكته في انتظار طابور المياه
سيجيء الشتاء قريباً
وأسطح المنزل غادرت
كيف سأقابلك الآن،
وأنا مبللة بالموت؟

غزة، ٢٠٢٤

I'll just organize my closet before I go.
Today, the sky above
the city is flying
and everyone is dancing on the edge.
Only those who've tasted the bullets will live.
I don't have a hot-air balloon.
I'll sip my coffee until the store runs out of beans.
I tell them I am okay.

So many amputated hands trying to shake mine.
The coffeepot shakes on the fire.
The funerals do not wait.
Is that the rain? Did it change direction?
A gravedigger, just wondering, looks up.

How many lemons are on the tree?
I'm spooked by the sparrows' panic.
By the sour smell of the season.
And the child, curly haired, crying,
who was not returned to his mother
after the church doors closed.

I have so much love in my heart.
I drained it waiting in the water line.
Winter will be here soon.
And all the rooftops have decamped.
And I have been drenched in death.
How will I meet you now.

Gaza, 2024

في المقهى

سيدة تبحث عن الظل، لا أحد يراها
النادل يساوم النهار ليحصل على مزيد من (البقشيش)
الوقت هنا مجرد سلعة.

في المقهى
الرجل الذي يقرأ الجريدة يبحث عن الكلمات المتقاطعة
الحرب والموت خبر قديم لا طائل من إعادة النظر إليه.

في المقهى
العتمة وهم وربما ملاذ
دائرة الضوء تسير باتجاه الفكرة
الجائع
الخائن
الأعمى
العاهر
السياسي
والمؤمن
الجميع هناك
كل يرى الانعكاس في الاتجاه الذي يخصه
حل الأحجية يأتي من حيث تشرق الشمس.

في المقهى
من يستطيع إمساك حقيقة الضوء؟
كيف نتعلم الحب والطائرات تحلق؟
نلون الورق
ثم نشد الخيط نحو علبة السكر الفارغة.

غزة، ٢٠٢٤

In the Café

A woman searches for shade. No one sees her.
A waiter bargains with the day for better tips.
Time is consumed in the café.

In the café, a man reads the paper, looking for a crossword.
War and death are old news, absurd
to revisit. In the café,

night is an illusion.
A circle of light expands toward some idea—
the hungry, the traitor, the blind, the debauched,

the politician, the devout,
each seeing their reflection from their own orientation.
The solution to this puzzle rises with the sun

in the café. Who can catch the truth light speaks of?
Who can learn love from these fighter jets?
We color in the paper. We tie a ribbon around
the empty sugar bowl.

Gaza, 2024

كيف نصنع حانة في البلاد الممنوعة من الحب

أرسم فما من نبيذ لامرأة تضع وشما أسفل ذقنها
و (تلدغ) في راءاتها المستديرة

في الحائط شق كبير . . . كانت تسكنه دالية عنب قديمة
لا حراس هنا

تسلق الأغصان واقطف آهاتها
ستسقط الشرفة وتصبح مزارا لسكارى الهوى

من أين لكزانوفا هذا الشبق وهو لم يشاهد أفلاما ممنوعة من العرض
كان يقف خلف الشاشة ليأخذ مشروبه طازجا ليصنع المشهد بنفسه

لعلك لا تعرفني أنا أيضا أزرع العنب والأفيون في حديقتي الخلفية
وحين تزهر القصائد أبيعها للعشاق في البلاد الممنوعة من الحب

إلى الرجل الأنيق بعيون عسلية زائدة السكر
رغم نظام الدايت الذي أتبعه
أريد أن أعلمك كيف تطهو تنهداتي على نار في العراء
هل تجيد صنع خيمة؟

إلى جاري الذي أراقب نافذته كل ليلة
عنوة بفستاني الضيق الذي أحب أن ألبسه
ابتسم
لتطعم الأطفال الأشقياء فطائر محلاة

إلى النساء اللواتي يحلقن لحاهن كل صباح
إلى ستائر الحمام الشفافة

How to build a pub in a country prohibited from love

I paint a mouthful of wine for a woman with a tattooed chin,
whose *r*'s have gone guttural.

In the wall, there's a large crevice where an old grapevine lives.

Climb its branches. Hear its sighs.
If the balcony plummets, you are in a shrine for those drunk on love.

And there are no guards here.

Casanova didn't watch banned films. Where did he get his desire?
He'd stand behind the screen, grab a fresh drink, then create a scene.

You might not know me, but I grow grapes and opium in my backyard,
and when poems bloom, I sell them to lovers in countries of forbidden love.

To the chic man with honey-colored eyes, sickly sweet—
despite my diet, I want to teach you to cook my moans over an open fire.
Will you make a tent?

To my neighbor whose window I peep through each night,
urged by the tight dress I love to wear,
I smile and feed
naughty children syruped pies.

To the women who shave their beards every morning,
to my transparent shower curtains,

لنفكر بحجة لقتل الملل . . .
اشنقي رجلا بقبلة دون سابق معرفة ثم افتحي مياه الاستحمام حتى يغرق العالم

إلى بائع (البوظة) وهو يراقب امرأة تلعق الآيس كريم كقطة شيرازي كسولة
ماذا لو لم يأت شباط؟

إلى الصور المخبأة تحت الوسائد
إلى عصفور يحاول نقر كرزة ذابت بين شفتي عاشقة
إلى بائع السجائر
كيف تستمرون بمشاهدة الأفلام الإباحية

إلى النساء اللواتي قدن الثورات بملابس داخلية زهرية اللون
إلى التفاحة التي تورطت بأمر الجاذبية
إلى عنب الخليل والنبيذ المحرم في الأقبية القديمة
إلى مخيلتي العابثة
كيف أعود للوقوف على رأسي . . . أقدامي متعبة؟

إلى الرجل «التئيل» تقال له بصوت لبناني مغناج
إلى شفاهه الغليظة التي تشبه سور برلين
الذي عبرت منه آلاف الشقروات العاشقات
إلى الحانات في عينيه وعنب الخليل المعتق
المرقي بصلوات الأمهات

إلى بائع الملابس النسائية
ورقصة الفلامنغو تهدي طرف التنورة الحمراء للريح
إلى العشاء الأخير
والموزة المعلقة بلاصق رخيص على الجدار

to the ice cream man watching a woman lick her soft-serve like a lazy Persian cat—
let's find an excuse, let's kill this boredom,
let's hang a stranger with a kiss then turn
the shower on until the world drowns
or February never comes.

To the pictures hidden under pillows,
to the sparrow trying to peck a berry softened
between some lover's lips,
to the cigarette seller,
how do you keep watching your porn?

To the women who led revolutions in pink panties,
to the apple that got caught up with gravity,
to Hebron's grapes and the forbidden wine of old cellars,
to my frivolous imagination,
how do I get back up on my tired feet?

To the tough guy, listen—a word whispered in a coquettish Lebanese accent.
To his full lips. They look like the Berlin Wall
thousands of blond lovers have passed through.
To the wine bars in his eyes, to the vintage grapes of Hebron
infused with mothers' Quranic recitations,

to the vendor of women's clothing,
and the flamenco dancer who dedicates the hem of her red skirt to the wind—
to the last supper,
to the banana duct-taped to a wall . . .

إلى الياقات البيضاء تعود بأحمر شفاه والكثير من الشتائم البذيئة
إلى مياه الاستحمام بعطور فرنسية تسيل لشهوة امرأة تعد الشوارع كل ليلة خوفا من العتمة
وصوت الكلاب البعيدة

إلى القط الشيرازي الذي يكره النساء ويجلس على قدمي عازف البيانو

إلى أناملك تبحث عن توبتها داخل كفي
إلى لحظات الجنون
الغزل
العصيان
وضربة مباغتة «رح نتفك»

إلى عطري وعطرك
إلى أسماء النساء في قلبك
إلى الفستان المغري على العارضة البلاستيكية
إلى غمزتك ذات المغزى
وإلى سائق الحافلة الذي لم ينتبه لقبلتك المسروقة ليدي

هل لكم أن تخبروني كيف أنظر لعينيه في منتصف الشارع
ولا أقول أحبك

غزة، ٢٠٢٤

To the white collars returning lipsticked with foul language.
To French-perfumed bathwater thirsting for a woman
who counts streets each night, afraid of darkness—to the distant barking of dogs.

And to the Persian cat who sits on the pianist's feet and hates women,

to your fingers searching for their repentance in my palm,
to disobedience,
to how I will screw you up,

to a sexy dress on a plastic mannequin,
to our perfumes,
to the names of all the women in your heart,
to that wink of yours,
to the bus driver who didn't notice your stolen kiss on my hand,
how can I not say "I love you"
when I look you in the eye, you in the middle of the street.

Gaza, 2024

سليمان الحزين

ذات مساء

ألا تعرفين
بماذا سأحلم عند المساءات؟
قالت سيأتيك طيفي
فقلت حنيني
كجميزة قد توالت عليها
رياح الخسارات
أنا يا ابنة الدمع
أحتاج خيلاً من البرق
يأخذ ناري وثأري
لآخر منفى
سأختار نوماً عميقاً
كطفل يلاحق ذيل المسافات
بقرب حقول الهدوء
سأختار غيماً
قريباً يلامس ورد
الخدود وعطر البنات
أريد سماء بدون
طيور الحديد التي
قتلت نسمة الفجر
بعد كل صلاة
بماذا سأختار ليلاً
أريد بلاداً
تصاحب ظلي
إذا كنت أمشي
وتسمع صوتي أقول أحبك
حتى الممات

Suleiman al-Hazeen

Just One Evening

Don't you already know
what I'll dream tonight?
You said, "My ghost will come visit you."
I replied, "My longing is
like a sycamore
buffeted by
winds of loss.
Daughter of tears, I
need lightning
to carry my fire, my vengeance,
down to the last exile.
I must choose a deep sleep
as a child pursues distant foothills,
near those tranquil fields.
I must choose clouds
nearby, just touching,
rose cheeks, and
women's perfume.
I want a sky free from these
iron birds
stifling the breeze
after every dawn prayer.
At night, what should I choose?
I want land
to escort my shadow through.
As I walk

وأصرخ لله يا رب
لقد شاب رأس الظلام
ونحن ننادي
نريد مساء
بلا راجمات
بلا مجرمين
ولا مجرمات
ولا طائرات
بلا ناقلات
بلا قاتلات

غزة، ٢٠٢٤

I hear my own voice say *I love you*
until death.
I cry, *Lord*
the darkness is turning gray.
We call and call again.
We want just one evening
without rocket launchers,
without criminals, without planes,
without tanks,
without murderers."
We want just one evening.

Gaza, 2024

عثمان حسين

شبعتُ موتاً

شبعت موتاً حتى امتلأتُ أنقاضاً ومفقودين
وحكاياتٍ لا تصلح للأحفاد الثكالى.
يا موتُ انتظرْ،
أحتاج أن أبلع ريقي،
أو حتى ينتهي الجلاد من أشغاله.
يا موت
أيها المُنادى،
لا تليق بنا.

أيها الكلب لا تنهش جثتي،
فأنا شهيد وكفى،
لا أعرف شيئاً عمّا أوصلني إلى هذا الوصف، ورضيتُ.
جعتُ مثلك أيها الوفي، لكنني لم أنهشك.
إياك إياك، فلعنتي ستسكن أحشاءك.
اترك جثتي تتحلل،
وامض جائعاً خير من لعنتي،
أيها الكلب الوفي.

غزة، ٢٠٢٤

Othman Hussein

I’m fed up with death

I’m fed up with death,
full of ruins and missing persons,
tales unfit for bereaved grandchildren.
O Death, wait!
At least, let me swallow my spit
first. Wait until the executioner’s done.
O Death—
you desired one,
you misfit.

As to you, dear dog,
don’t maul my corpse.
I’m martyr enough,
and I don’t even know why.
But I’m content.
I go hungry, like you, O loyal one,
and I don’t eat you.
Beware, friend.
My curse’ll haunt
your intestines.
So let my dead body decompose.
Do not approach it.
Better to go hungry
than be cursed,
O dear, faithful dog.

Gaza, 2024

لعنة

أشقُّ اللحظةَ بمبضع لا يصلحُ للجراح
تتقافز الوجوه مأخوذةً بالشهيق
أخيطُ الجرح وأبتسمُ للعصيّ التي تتكسَّر على رؤوس الأشهاد
أشقُّها كي أُؤجّل رزمة الأحلام عاماً آخر
مرةً خيّرتها بين فصلين فاجرين
فجاءتِ الحربُ من أول النهار
جاءتْ شتيمةً سوداء
أكلتْ لحمنا
لم تترك للجائعين غَيْرَ حسراتٍ وأحلامٍ أفسدها الانتظارُ.

غزة، ٢٠٢٤

A Curse

Bisecting the moment with a blunt scalpel—
faces leap and plunge, barely breathing.
I stitch the wound. I won't acknowledge the canes that break
over our heads in public.
I cut the moment open
to delay its dream-bundle
one more year. Give us one more.
Later, I say, choose between these two
ungodly terms. From the first day, the war
arrived as curse, ate at our bodies.
It left nothing for the hungry
but heartbreak. The dream that rots from waiting.

Gaza, 2024

ملل

إلى الشاعرة سميرة أحمد

الملل يطفو على رغوة السؤال
والوقت ينبح خلفي حين أجرجر بقاياه،
مع ذيل نعاسي.
ستنجو تلك الدقائق التي أكلت ورق النعناع،
هذا الوقت الذي يطل ويغطس هناك،
على مرمى عويل العقارب
البحر غارق في صمتي،
وتلك الدقائق التي قفزت من معطفي
ستنجو من الغرق.
تنبت الأسئلة في حوض الوقت،
وترتوي من حوارك البارد.
تحمل الصقيع على كتفيك

فتزهر بلورات ثلج من رؤوس الكلمات.
تلك الدوائر التي ضاقت واعتصرت حبات الروح أغرقتني،
طفتُ حولك مشدوهة
في حضرة الكلام
تنتصب الحواس على أقدامها حافية.

غزة، ٢٠٢٤

To Boredom

for the poet Samira Ahmed

Tedium floats on the foam of inquiry,
time barks behind me as I drag its remains
by the tail of my lethargy.
Those minutes that nibbled mint leaves will survive.
This era floats up and nose-dives
at the sight of howling scorpions.
The sea drowns in my quiet,
but those moments that jump from my coat pocket
escape.
Questions germinate in the tin basin of time,
watered by our cold conversation.
You collect frost on your shoulders.
Ice crystals spiral from the tips of your words.
They narrow and squeeze my soul,
they sink me.
And I circle you, floating, mesmerized.
We're in the presence of language.
The senses all rise to their bare feet.

Gaza, 2024

قسمتي من الأحلام

تلك الليلة، حلمتُ أن الخراف في بلادي هللت للرجال الذين لم يأخذوها في طريقهم إلى مسلخ غزة الشهير. اعتدلتُ، أمسكت كبشاً فتياً، ألقيته خارج الحلم، فصحوتُ. لا أدري كيف أمضيتُ ليلتي، في حلم يتعثر أمام تفاصيله، يتقطع، ويقطع غفوتي بنصل يأكله الصدأ. لكنني أمضيتها طافياً على سطح النعاس، تتلاطمني هزَّات تتفجر من قاعٍ مجهولة، إلى أن صحوت مرة أخرى على همسات بهية: بابا اصحا، اتأخرتْ، فيْ حربْ.

لولا أن أحلامنا تتوزع بيننا كأرزاق لا يعلمها الجيران عن جيرانهم، ولولا أن تفاصيلها تدفع الشغف إلى رؤوس الحالمين، لرفضت قسمتي، والتي، كالعادة، لا تعدو عن حلم أفسده التكرار، لن أقبل بعد اليوم حلماً لا يتحدى كابوساً.

أيتها الأحلام الشجاعة، لا يعجبني الحلم المتردد في الكشف عن حلميته.
في ليلة ما، بنيت حلماً وسكنته، زينت له المنخفضات والوديان، كنت أخشى عليه من السقوط.
انظري يا رفيقتي، هذا الفضاء الذي لا تشبعه الأكوان، يقتات على أحلام راكمها صمتُ الحالمين.
احلمي إذن يا نغم، فالأحلام تحرك العالم، ولا تجعلي مصيرها السقوط في مستنقع الكوابيس.

غزة، ٢٠٢٤

My Share of Dreams

That night, I saw sheep greeting the men who didn't take them to Gaza's slaughterhouse, so I grabbed a ram by the horns, stood up straight, and threw him from the dream, then woke up. I don't know how I spend the night, in visions, stumbling over details, and blacked-out beside a rusted blade. But that night I floated on drowsiness, tossed by tremors erupting from depths, until I was roused by happy whispers: *Daddy, wake. It's late. There's the war.*

If it weren't that dreams like provisions are secretly distributed among us, without our neighbors knowing, their residues surging into passions then into the dreaming heads, if it weren't for this, I would renounce my share, which is always only a dream repetition won't fulfill . . . After today, I won't admit a dream that doesn't fly into the face of nightmares.

Brazen dreams—I don't like those which hesitate to bare their hearts.
One night I built a dream and moved entirely into it. I decorated it with plains and valleys. I was afraid it would collapse.
Look, my friend, at this insatiable space even universes can't fill. It feeds on reveries stored up in dreamers' reticence.
Sleep then, dear Nagham, move the world, don't let your dreams drop into the mire of this night's terrors.

Gaza, 2024

هناء العمصي

النار تحرق المسافة

مال لهذا الخراب لا يبرحني
والوقت يقضم وجهي كالتفاحة قبل سقوط آدم.
يفرد أجنحته على ظهري الأحدب
فلا سماء أحلق بها
ولا سحاب يمطرني أملاً
مال هذا الحزن بكل مكرٍ
يلقي التحية على عيوني
الباكية.
يعبر ضجيج روحي
ويفترش المكان بصمت
يمزق جسدي كالخرقة البالية.
هذا المساء لم يترفق
بقلبي اليتيم.
لم ينصت ولو مرة لعويل الذئاب فوق سماء غزة
لم يتمهل وهو يمسح بأنامل فولاذية
على جبين أطفالي الوردي.
يبكون صباحاً كالعصافير الوحيدة في جحور النسور.
عام يمر وأنا أجلس على قارعة الموت.
أحاول عبور جسر الضياع ولو مرة.
كلما رأيت الموت يرقص كالمهرّج
على جدرانٍ المدارس والمخيمات.
الحياة أفرغت جرابها من أنفاسنا المتسارعة.

Hana al-Imsi

Fire burns up distance

Time spreads its wings over my hunched back.
Time bites at my face like the apple of Adam's fall.
Why won't these ruins leave me.
But the sky has been erased,
clouds won't shower down hope,
grief inclines cunningly.
It greets me where I weep.
It passes over the uproar of my soul.
It's silently conquering this place,
tearing my tattered rag, my body.
Once again, this evening won't be kind.
Dear orphaned heart,
don't hear the dogs howl over Gaza,
don't pause to wipe its steely fingers
over my children's foreheads.
And in the mornings, don't make them cry, these lonely sparrows in eagles' nests.
A year passes. I stand on the verge of death.
I try to cross this bridge of loss.
I see death dance like a clown
over the school walls, through the camps,
through these days whose ashes remain in the mouth of the wind,
these hearts going gray, these jerking limbs,

فأصبح الوقت بقايا رماد في فوهة الريح.
تشيب القلوب و تفزع الجوارح
كلما عوى صوت الصدى
يشق سكون الليل،
أحلم بالبقاء.
طالما حلمت بالحياة والبقاء.

غزة، ٢٠٢٤

these echoes howling, splitting the still night.
Now life empties its bag of our quickening breaths.
I dream of survival. I have always dreamed of survival.

Gaza, 2024

هند جودة

تقرع الطبول

تقرعُ الطبول
تُرهقُ سمع الهواء
تُفسدُ مذاق الفم
تُحطِّمُ النهار
تحوّلُ المدن إلى أكوام حجارة
والملابس النظيفة إلى حلم.

الطبولُ لا تتوقف عن التهام السماء
والإنسان ما زال يكرّر بشاعته!
يشعل ناراً
لها رأسٌ ووزن
لها صوت صراخ
ورائحة فزع.

تقرع طبولٌ في بلادي
يستيقظ الليل ناسياً غفوته
يلملم ما قد يطفو من أنفاس مطفأة
تلسعه أصابعه
يفتح الكفن الفارغ
ويجمع الأشلاء الناجية.

لم يعد مسموحاً أن تحلم بعلمٍ يخفق
أنت مجرّد حيوان بشريّ
لا طابور في الحرب سوى لملء الماء
ربما لانتظار الخبز أو الأرز المسلوق!

Hind Joudeh

Drums

The drumming starts,
the air strains to hear it.
It leaves a bad taste.
It tears the day apart. It breaks
the city into an avalanche.
Only dreams can clean these clothes.

The drumming won't stop,
it consumes the sky.
Man is monstrous.
He builds his fire,
with mass and a head,
the scent of panic,
a screaming sound.

Drums beat in my country.
Night wakes, forgets rest,
grabs what floats on lifeless breath.
Its fingers burn,
they tear at an empty shroud,
they collect the remains.

You are only a human animal
queuing for water.
Perhaps there'll be bread.
Perhaps there will be boiled rice.

هل يشتاق طفلك لحقيبة الظهر والكتب؟
هل يتآكلُ خوفاً؟
هل يبكي حزناً على معلم مقتول؟
لن تسمعه حربٌ لا تجد وقتاً للأطفال الباكين
إنها تقرع طبولها!

غزة، ٢٠٢٤

Your child still wants a backpack of books.
How much of him has fear devoured?
Does he mourn his murdered teacher?
War beats on its drum. It keeps on beating.
It tunes its deaf ear to the screaming of children.

Gaza, 2024

رأساً على عقب

عن مدينة ألعاب تحولت إلى مأوى للنازحين في الحرب
المدينة مطفأة،
لا كاميرات ترصد خوفها وعتمتها من البنايات العالية
قُضمتْ البنايات من أعناقها،
أو سقطت مغشياً عليها!
لم يعد شيء مثلما كان في الشوارع الأليفة،
صرنا مثل قططٍ مشرّدة،
ننتظر طعاماً لا نطهوه،
ونشرب الماء في العلب الفارغة
لا كؤوس ماء براقة،
لا طقم ملاعق متشابه،
لا أغطية نختارها حسب الذوق،
لا فراش يليق بجسد متعب،
أجزاء من أمتار قليلة يحيط بها القماش
لا جدران ولا دورة مياه خاصّة!
كم تبدو تلك الـ (خاصة) جارحةً ومضحكة!
لا شيء هنا يشبه البيت
أفرغت البيوت من أنفاسها،
وقُلبتْ مثل وجبة البلاد التقليدية رأساً على عقب.

كم من طفلٍ خائف وحزين في الخيام الآن؟
كلهم ينظرون إليكِ كوحشٍ وحيدٍ قادرٍعلى جعلهم يصرخون منتشين من الفرح
دوري أيتها الأرجوحة،
لا كهرباء في المدينة أيتها الشقية.

غزة، ٢٠٢٤

Upside Down

An-Noor Amusement Park is switched off.
Cameras don't catch the glinting of its Ferris wheel.
The towers are bitten off at the neck. They have
blacked out. Now like stray cats we
wait for food we didn't cook,
we drink water from emptied cans—
no glimmering glasses of water,
no matching spoons, no mattresses,
no pretty throws for worn-out bodies.
Just this piece of cloth.
No walls, no restrooms.
What a mockery "privacy" would be. How quaint.
This is not home—
houses had the breath knocked out of them—
like our *maqluba,* turned upside down.

Everywhere these fearful, mournful children in camps now.
They all look at you, you lonely monster once able to make them
scream with glee.
Swing—oh swing higher—they once cried
to you, Delinquent Park. Now where is your power.

Gaza, 2024

قدم صغيرة

ليست قطعة ثلجٍ،
وإن بدت باردةً مثله.
لم تعد تركض،
لأنها لم تتعلم المشي بعد.
ليست وردة،
لكنني أشمّها مثل ورد.
ليست وجهاً،
لكنني أقبّلها مثل خدّ.
ليس دمعاً،
نشف ماء عيني منذ احترق قلبي.
لست حياً،
فأنا أختنق.
لست ميتاً،
لكنها روحي ترتعش مثل طائر مذبوح!

تقفز الأسئلة من قاعك،
تصطدم بكل شيء،
وتعود إليك دائخةً، ضريرة!

لم يعد للرتابة وقتٌ
إنها أيام لا تمرّ،
عرجاء إن سارت،
غائمةٌ تمطر القلق
ما أصعب أن نجهل،
ما أوجع أن نعرف
ما أقسى أن نشكّ،

A Little Foot

Not a patch of snow.
Though as cold.
No longer runs.
Didn't learn to walk.
Not a rose, that wound.
I breathe it in.
Not a face.
Like a cheek. I kiss it.

My heart
dried my eyes.
I'm not alive—I'm choking.
I'm not dead.
What is this soul quivering,
a dying bird,
mind perched above your habitat—
what have you done with your hidden wings—
crashing into everything,
dizzy and blind.

Days do not pass,
they limp beneath
anguish-laden clouds.
It's hard not to know.
It's painful to know.
Doubt is cruel.

و أن ننتظر فوق جسر الهاوية.
تدورُ علينا كؤوسٌ الخيبة على شكل أخبار عاجلة.
والبشرية مغشيٌّ عليها.

غزة، ٢٠٢٤

Waiting on a bridge. Hung over a chasm.
Cups of disappointment being passed around
as breaking news:
Humankind is losing
consciousness.

Gaza, 2024

خالد جمعة

حين يغادر الجنودُ المكان

حين يغادرُ الجنودُ المكان
سأخرجُ . . . لأشتري لك بضعة ملليمترات من الهواء
وأحاولُ-إن استطعت-أن أغني لكِ
كي تنامي
فأنتِ لستِ ابنتي، أعرف ذلك
لكنني أستطيع أن أكون أباكِ
ويمنعني الجنودُ من ذلك!

حين يغادرُ الجنودُ المكان
لا تكترثي بكل تلك الأشجار المحروقة
ولا بكل تلك الأعمار المحروقة
أو بتلك الأماني المحروقة
بل اتّكئي على كتفي
وحاولي بقدمك الوحيدة

أن تسيري الخطوات العشرين
التي تفصل البيت
عن بائع الحلوى

حين يغادرُ الجنودُ المكان
قولي لي ما كان يمنعك منه الخوف
أظهري دمعكِ ساخناً وملوّناً بقليل من الكحل
لن يلومك أحد على هذا
فجميعهم، قبل أن يأتوا ليتأكدوا أنك ما زلت حيةً . . .
قد بكوا شيئاً ما، وتماسكوا . . .

Khaled Juma

When the Soldiers Leave This Place

When the soldiers leave this place,
I'm going out to buy a few millimeters of air
and try, if I can, to sing you
to sleep.
You are not my daughter, I know that.
But I can be your father.
The soldiers won't let me.
They do not permit it.

When the soldiers leave this place,
turn a blind eye to these burned trees,
all those burned years,
these burned wishes.
Lean on my shoulder,
and with your one foot, try
to walk the twenty steps
that separate our rooms
from the one who sells candy.

When the soldiers leave this place,
tell me, from what did fear keep you?
Show your tears.
Nobody blames you for this.
Everybody when they came to check
if you were still alive,
cried out, held on.

حين يغادرُ الجنودُ المكان
لا تغيّري وجهة نظركِ في الأشياء
الصورةُ المخزوقةُ بالرصاص

هي الصورة ذاتها
والمرآة التي كسرها كعب بندقية
هي المرآة التي كنتِ تتأكدين من جديلتيك عليها
وتزعجينني وأنا أنتظر
كي أوصلك إلى المدرسة
وقطّتُكِ السمينة تلك
أقصد التي تحوّلت إلى قطة ميتة
حين رفسها جنديٌّ بحذائه العسكري
هي القطة ذاتها
كل ما في الأمر يا حبيبتي
أن الجنود كانوا هنا . . .

حين يغادرُ الجنودُ المكان
سنضحك من ذلك الجندي الذي غالبه النعاس
فأطلق رصاصةً على الثلاجةِ
بعد أن صرخ عليه القائد فاستيقظ
فالجنودُ بشرٌ مثلنا
لكن الفرق بيننا وبينهم
أننا نحملُ كارثةً على ظهورنا
وهم يحملون بنادق في أعينهم
وتوراةً في أرواحهم

حين يغادرُ الجنودُ المكان
لا تعبثي بما خلفوه من الروايات
فهم يعرفون أنهم لا يعرفون سوى ما يعرّفونهم إياه

When the soldiers leave this place,
don't change.
The photograph shot through with bullets
is the same photograph.

And the mirror shattered by a rifle butt
is the mirror in which you checked your braids
while I waited,
impatient, to take you to school.
And your fat kitten,
I mean, your dead kitten,
kicked by a soldier's boot,
is the same kitten.
It is only, my beloved, that those soldiers were here . . .

When the soldiers leave this place,
we'll laugh over the officer who, dozing off,
hearing his commander shout,
fired a bullet into the fridge then woke up.

Soldiers are human like us,
but we carry catastrophe on our backs.
They have guns for eyes,
the Torah twists in their souls.

When the soldiers leave this place
don't mess with what remains of the story.
They know—they only know
what is only known to them.

وذلك الكيس الذي سقط من خاصرة الجندي الأخير
ليس بالضرورة أن يكون كيس حلوى
فكثيراً ما يُسقط الجنود
أكياساً من الخُبث العسكري
ويبتهجون كثيراً حين تنطلي الحيلةُ
على المسالمين

حين يغادرُ الجنودُ المكان
سنقف أنا وأنتِ
ونقرأُ ما كتبوه على جدران بيتنا
ونضحك كثيراً
لأنهم أخطأوا في كتابة الحروف
فهم لا يعرفون لغتنا
لأن من علّمهم إياها
لم يكن يعرفها كذلك.

غزة، ٢٠٢٢

And that bag that fell from the soldier's belt
may not contain candy.
They often drop bags.
They cheer when the trick works.
Don't touch it.

When the soldiers leave this place
you and I will stand up
and read what they wrote on the walls of our house
and laugh—
look, they misspelled some words.
They don't know our language.
Whoever taught them,
they didn't learn.

Gaza, 2022

بنت من القدس

على القباب القريبة من القلب كنتُ ألهو، بعد أن خبّأتني الأشجار ألف قرنٍ في نوى ثمارها، أعدو في ساحات المدينةِ مثل جندبٍ حرٍّ في حقلٍ مهجور، تتلألأ التلال في عينيّ، وأعبرُ الأزمان في فرحٍ أسطوريٍّ وجنونِ طفلةٍ عاديّةٍ لا يقلقها وقتٌ أو جيوشٌ غريبةْ.

تناسختُ في كلّ بنتٍ رسمت العالم بطبشورةٍ من حجارة المدينة، كنت أنا التي لعبت على الأسوار لعبة الأم التي تحمي أولادها من الهواء البارد، لم يكن هناك ما يؤرّق قلبي الصغير، كان ذلك قبل أن يخترعوا الأخبارَ، وقبل أن أعرف أن القداسةَ مُرّةٌ، وأن بيتي مطلوبٌ من حضارات الأرض وإمبراطورياتها العظيمة، سكنتني الأرواح التي من حبٍّ ففتحتُ ذراعيّ لمن أرادوا الصلاة في أقربِ نقاط الأرض إلى الله، لم أكن ساذجةً حين ضممتهم إلى قلبي وأعلنتُ أن مدينتي مدينتهم، لكنهم لم يفهموا مجازاتي، وحاصروا فتنتي في زاوية ضيقةٍ من السور القديم، وكلّما اخترعوا سلاحاً، جرّبوه في قلبي.

كمن يأتي من حقول الريح أتوا، بلا ملامح تشبهني، بلا آثار أصابعهم على الطرقات والحيطان، جرحوا الرّملَ والجبل، جرحوا حياض الماءِ وجففوا ذاكرة الأمكنة، كلُّ جرحٍ في جلدهم غطّوه بجثة ولدٍ لم يعرف عن مأساتهم حرفاً، وبقيتُ كي أروي مأساتي التي لم يسمعها أحد، هاربةً في الحقول الخضراء المملوءة بالدمع، صلبوني كي يبنوا ألعاب أولادهم في خاصرتي.

كنتُ طفلةً سعيدةً، لم أفهم ألم التاريخ، قلتُ: لم أؤذِ أحداً، فلن يؤذيني أحد، هكذا يفكرُ الأطفالُ السعداءُ عادةً، لكني الآن الطفلة التي كبّرها الوجعُ، وتحاولُ أن تفهمَ كيفَ تحوّل الليلُ الجميلُ إلى وحشِ حكاياتِ الرعب تلك، أن تفهم لماذا تقصُّ أسنانُ الجرّافةِ ما تبقى لي من حلمٍ قديم، أن تفهم ما تعنيه مفردة الأعداء، فلم يكن لي من عدوٍّ سوى النوم الذي يمنعني من احتضانِ المدى، وما زلت ألملمُ حكاية جدّاتي، في كيس القلب، وأجفّف القصب من أجل النايات، فالأولادُ يحبّون الحكاية أكثر إذا رافقها ناي.

أطلّ من المدينة على المدينة، من البلاد على البلاد، كلّ أولئك الذين ماتوا وتدحرجت أرواحهم إلى هنا، عرفوا ربما بعد أن أكلتهم النهايات، أن الليل يأخذ وقته ويمضي، وأن النهار يأخذ وقته كذلك ويمضي، لكنهم لم يقولوا ذلك لأحد، ولم يعترفوا أن بيتي الذي كان مفتوحاً للذين مزّقتهم الخرافةُ،

A Girl from Jerusalem

After trees hid me for a thousand centuries in their fruits' pits, I played on the domes near the heart, I leaped through city squares like a grasshopper free in deserted fields, hills shimmering in my eyes, crossing ages with the legendary joy of an ordinary child's madness, unpuzzled by time or strange armies.

I'm reincarnated in every girl who's drawn the world with the chalk of city stones, I was that girl playing mom on the walls, guarding her kids from cold, nothing clutched my little heart. This was before news was invented, and I learned that the holy is bitter or my house is coveted by Earth's great civilizations. I was inhabited by souls of love, opened my arms to anyone who wanted to pray where the earth is closest to God. I wasn't naive, embracing them, declaring my city their city. They didn't fathom my metaphors. They surrounded me in a narrow corner of the old wall. And when they invented a weapon, they tried it out on my heart.

As if descending from windfields, they came, without features like mine, without fingerprints on walls and streets, they wounded the sand and mountains, wounded the springs, dried up places' memories, held the corpse of a boy who knew nothing of their catastrophe, and I stayed to tell of my Nakba. No one hears. Escaping through green fields, filled with tears, no one hears.

A happy girl, knowing nothing of history's nightmare, I said, I won't harm anyone, no one'll harm me. That's how happy children think. How did the pretty night turn into a horror story, a monster, the bulldozer's teeth ripping remnants of old dreams—what does the word *enemies* mean? I had no enemy but the sleep that stopped me embracing the expanse. But I still collect my grandma's tales in the heart bag, dry the reeds. Children most love the stories accompanied by flute.

قد أغلقوه على أنفسهم ووضعوني في جنون الريح، أطرقُ بابي حتى تدمى يدي، ولا يفتح لي أحد، يا الله . . . كيف صاروا هناك وصرتُ هنا؟

لم يعترفوا بأنني بنيتُ كل هذه المعابد التي يتقربون بها إلى الله، وكل هذه الجدران التي تحمي البشرية من السقوط، وأنني ألّفت كل هذه الأغاني التي تعيد للعالم اتّزانه، وكل هذه الرقصات التي تأتي بالمطر وتعين الثمار على النضوج . . .

سأنضجُ أكثر كلّما مرّ صيفٌ على الحواري الضيّقة، سأقيمُ بيتي فيّ، أحمله كلّما نخزوا خصري كي يبعدوني عني، سأذكّر أولادي بالمذبحة، وبكرومي التي أخجَلَت الصحاري، سأفكُّ شرائط شعري الملوّنةَ وأربط بها خصر المدينة إلى الأبد.

غزة، ٢٠٢٢

I look on this city from the city, on this country from the country. I look on all those who died, whose souls rolled here, who knew, having been eaten by ends, that the night takes its time then passes, that the day takes its time then passes. Don't tell anyone but they locked themselves in my house. They left me out in the wind's insanity. I knocked on the door till my hands bled, and no one opened it. God, how did they get there, and me here?

They won't tell you I built these temples where they worship God, these walls guarding humanity from falling, these songs to balance the world, these dances to conjure rain and ripen fruits. With each summer that passes through my narrow neighborhood I come of age, I build my house within me, I carry it when they hit me in the guts, separating me from me. I will remind my children of the massacre and the vines that shamed the desert. I will loosen my colorful ribbons. I will fasten them about the city's waist forever.

Gaza, 2022

رغيف واحد

منذ عشرة أيام
أبحث عن رغيف واحد
رغيف واحد، لا أكثر
قالوا لي إنه اختفى في المخازن الدولية
طفل أخبرني أنه شاهده يصعد خشبة المسرح
التي قصفتها الطائرات.

الرغيف مراوغ، وقدماي متعبتان
لكن أولادي الصغار لا يفهمون ذلك
يظنّون أنهم في الزمن القديم
حين كانوا يأكلون وقتما جاعوا
ويفكّرون في الخطأ الذي ارتكبوه
كي أعاقبهم بالجوع والعطش
آخر جملةٍ قالها لي أصغرهم صباحاً:
أليس هذا عقاب مبالغ فيه يا أبي؟

غزة، ٢٠٢٤

Just a Loaf

For ten or so days
I've been searching for a loaf,
just a loaf.
They said it vanished from global warehouses.
A child saw it take to the stage,
or was it bombed by a plane.

The loaf is elusive, and my feet are tired.
My little ones don't understand,
they think they're in the old days,
you ate whenever you got hungry,
they wonder what they did wrong,
why do I punish them with this hunger and this thirst.
The last thing my youngest says to me this morning—
isn't this too much punishment, Dad?

Gaza, 2024

حفار قبور

عملتُ في عشرة بلدان
حفاراً للقبور
كانت لدي كل الوقت
مجرفةٌ صغيرةٌ أعلقها في حزامي
وأمضي بها كميدالية كبيرة بعض الشيء.
تسعةٌ من هذه البلاد
كان كل شيء فيها طبيعياً:
ميتٌ كل أسبوع
اثنان على الأكثر.

قلتُ: سأتقاعد في مدينةٍ على البحر
وجئت هنا، أعني إلى غزة.
لم تعد مجرفتي تعني شيئاً،
اشتريت آلةً صغيرةً
ثم حفّاراً
ووظفتُ جميع العاطلين عن العمل «حفاري قبور».
كل هذا لم يكفِ
فأسستُ شركةً للموت
هي الأولى في بورصة العالم
إلى اليوم.

غزة، ٢٠٢٤

The Gravedigger

I've worked in ten countries
as a gravedigger.
A little shovel hung off my belt.
I walked about with it. A medallion.
In nine of those countries,
things were normal.
One dead a week
or two, no more.

I said, I'll retire to a city by the sea.
And I came here, to Gaza.
Now my shovel is useless.
I bought a little digger,
then an excavator,
hired all the unemployed.
Still, it's not enough.
I have built a business with death.
Now we are first on the stock exchange.
Second to none.

Gaza, 2024

عندما تنتهي الحرب

عندما تنتهي الحرب
لن أكتب أسماء الشهداء على ألواح مرمرية
سأدفنهم بما يليق بهم
وأشربُ نسيانهم لأنظف ذاكرتي
ربما أبكي قبل بداية النسيان
ربما أشتم شيئاً مجهولاً
وأكز على أسناني في فورة غضب
وأترك الجرحى ينزفون على الأرض
لأني مشغول بالبكاء عليهم
لكني سأنسى، كالوطن الذي لا ذاكرة له
فلو كان يملك ذاكرة
لما استطاع أن يحيا بكل هؤلاء الشهداء فيها.

عندما تنتهي الحرب
سأعود إلى طبيعتي
سأشطب أرقام أصدقائي الذين ماتوا
عن جهازي الخلوي
سأنزع صورهم من الألبومات
حتى تلك التي أنا فيها معهم
سأنسى أسماءهم وأستبدلهم بأصدقاء أحياء
وسأتحرر من هداياهم، لوحاتهم، قصائدهم، أغانيهم
ولا بأس إن أخذوا قطعةً من قلبي
فالحياة بربع قلبٍ ممكنة.

عندما تنتهي الحرب
لن أزور البنايات المهدمة
ولا الأماكن التي ربيت فيها ذكرياتي

When the War Is Over

When the war is over
I won't carve the martyrs' names on headstones.
I will bury them with dignity.
I will drink to their oblivion.
I will drink to cleanse myself of memory.
Perhaps I will cry before the forgetting begins.
What a strange fragrance,
then this grinding of teeth.
I leave the wounded to bleed into the earth,
I am too busy crying over them.
But soon I will forget. I will forget the way a country forgets
in order to outlive its martyrs.

When the war is over
I will return to my old habits.
I will delete my dead friends' numbers
from my contacts.
I will remove their photos from my album.
I will forget their names. Swap them with those of living friends.
Please free me from their gifts—their paintings, their poems, their songs.
It is possible to live with one-quarter of a heart.

When the war is over
I won't visit the disappeared buildings.
What good is memory without place?
I will swat them away from my soul, buzzing houseflies.
I will grow new memories

فماذا ستنفع الذكريات بلا أمكنة؟
سأهشُّها كذبابة غبيّةٍ عن روحي
وأربي ذكرياتٍ جديدة
على صفحةٍ بيضاء
وربما أؤلّفُ ذكرياتٍ كما يحلو لي
فمن سيحاسبني وقد اختفت الأمكنةُ والأشخاص
سأكون في الذكرياتِ ولداً سعيداً
لم يشهد حرباً في حياته
ولم يُقتل أقرباءه في الحرب
بل لا يعرفُ معنى كلمة حرب
سأرتب ذكريات عائلتي كذلك
وبلادي
وسأصير من بلادٍ لم تشهد قتلاً
منذ ألف قرن.

حين تنتهي الحرب
لن أنتبه إلى الأطفال الخائفين
سأعتبر أن خوفهم سوء تربية
وأن ارتجافهم مرضاً عصبياً
وأن بكاءهم دلعاً زائداً عن الحد
وأنهم حين ظلوا وحيدين دون أهلهم
ذلك لأنهم أولاد فاسدون
يهربون من البيت
حتى أنهم ما عادوا يعرفون طريق البيت
من كثرة ما هربوا.

عندما تنتهي الحرب
لن أبحث عن قبر حبيبتي
ولن أكتب شعراً فيها

on this blank page.
I will compose memories as I please.
Who would judge me?
See, in my memory I am now a happy child,
who never saw a war in his life,
who doesn't know what *war* means.
Whose family isn't murdered.
Let me reinvent their memories too.
Let them come from a country that hasn't seen a killer
for a thousand millennia.

When the war is over
I won't pay attention to the frightened children.
I will say their fear is a sign of bad parenting.
Or maybe they tremble from some neurological disorder.
Or cry from mollycoddling.
When they are parentless
it's only because they were naughty—
they ran away from home.
They can't even remember the way home.
They've run away so many times.

When the war is over
I won't search for my lover's grave.
I won't write poems about her.
I'll pretend I left her. That I didn't love her.
I will criticize her hair,
I will criticize the way she spoke—
her eyelids drooping when she said *I love you.*

سأدّعي أنني تركتُها لأنها لم تعجبني
سأنتقد تسريحةَ شعرِها
وطريقتها في الكلام
وذبول عينيها حين تقول: أحبك
سأقول إنني لأجل هذا تركتُها
فهاجرت إلى بلادٍ بعيدة
وحين يسألني فضوليّ عن الكلام المكتوب على قبرها
سأقول: مجرد تشابه في الاسم والعمر لا أكثر
وسأهرب قبل أن يسألني
ماذا تفعل هنا إذن؟

غزة، ٢٠٢٤

I will say *That is why I left her*
and then she emigrated. Far away.
And when that curious man asks what is written on that grave,
I will say *It is just a coincidence of name and age. Nothing more.*
And I'll leave before he asks
But then what are you doing here?

Gaza, 2024

نبال خليل

يا آدم

يا آدم
تصحرت روحي
أخرج من جنتكَ
كما خرجت حواء
أنت أغويتها

وأنا أتناسخ اليوم عنها
تدلف روحي رملاً
ليس لجوف الأرض جنة
ها أنا أتيبّس مثل يوروديس
ينحلُّ ضلعي المنخلع منك
أسلخكَ الآن من جلدي
شكلتني من وحل والآن أخرجك اليوم من وحل.

لا تقرّب مساميرك من مغناطيسي
قطبان سالبان يتنافران
صدئ وجهك
واحدودبت أفكارك
لم يعد لطوافي حولك بقية
اجتزتُ دوائرك المنسوجة بخيوط عنكبوت.

Nibal Khalil

O Adam

O Adam,
my soul is drying.
What are you doing still in your paradise.
Get out. Eve did.
You seduced her.

Today I will be reborn from her,
my soul will sink into sand,
into Earth's hollow where there's no paradise.
Like Euridice, I will petrify.
My rib will dislocate
from you. I will strip you from
my skin. You formed me
from clay and now I will scrape you
out of it.

Don't let your iron filings
near my magnet.
Your face is rusted.
Your thoughts have dulled.
I no longer revolve around you,
I pass through your cobwebbed spirals.

سأتجه شمالاً لأراك أصبحت جليداً لا ينحسر
فارتقي بي دون فزع
جثة متحركة بعد معركة دون حلم
فلن تراني ولن ترى زوّاري.

الضفة الغربية، ٢٠٢٤

I am heading north to see
you freeze. This frost won't recede.
You will rise with me—
a corpse walking from a dreamless battle.
You won't notice me or my guests.

West Bank, 2024

حياة

وتبدو الحياة بكامل أناقتها
تأكل أطراف العمر بأسنانها الماسيّة
وتبصق على ما تبقّى من الأحلام
و تهديني الطريق بلا خارطة في يميني
تبكي عليّ في المحطة دون دمع
وتلوّح لي عند آخر كرسي أن أصعد القطار،

فأقف مثل صنم في وسط القطار
أراني في المرايا السائلة من حولي وهي تحاصرني
أرى ما تبقّى من صور
وأصرخ بكل صمتي على نهر الزمن.

الضفة الغربية، ٢٠٢٣

Life

Today life is in fashion again.
Diamond teeth gnaw at its limbs, at its extremities,
spitting on dream-remnants.
Life points to the road. I've no map in my hand.
Now life's crying for me at the station without tears.
It waves to me from the last open seat. Get on board.

I stand stunned in this aisle.
I see myself in the molten mirrors. They surround me.
What remains of the visible?
This is when my silent screaming into the river of time begins.
This is when the devouring grief begins.

West Bank, 2023

محمد الخطيب

أو ما تعبت؟

من أي أغنية أتيت
تتكرر الأشياء فيك
وتعزف نايات القصب أحلامي
وترتحل الدروب بكل ما فيها إليك
لا زلت أرتشف الأسى
وأنام فوق وسادة الجرح المزخرف
باعتذارات المساء
يا قلب تشتعل الحرائق في دمي
أو ما تعبت؟
من أي نافذة أتيت
من أي موت
كل الدروب تعد أنفاسي اليك
إذا أتيت
فبأي صوت
سوف أعلن عن حضوري؟
أي صوت
غاب الصهيل من الخيول
وغبت أنت
وسرجت من وجعي طقوسك
والمساء ترنّحت خطواته
وأنا على كل المنافذ
أسأل الطرقات عنك

غزة، ٢٠٢٤

Mohammad al-Khatib

Are You Not Tired Yet?

From which song did you arise?
You're repeating yourself.
Reed flutes play in my dream.
All paths (and everything on them) travel to you.
I still sip the sorrow.
I sleep on the embroidered wound of a pillow.
I sleep under the evening's apologies.
My blood is on fire,
aren't you too tired yet?
In which window did you appear?
From which death did you emerge?
Each step down the path counts my breath.
If I arrive,
in what tone
should I announce myself?
In what voice?
I can't hear the horses' neighing.
You vanished.
I saddled your routines with my mourning.
But the night staggers on.
I stand at each entrance.
I ask the streets about you.

Gaza, 2024

يسرى الخطيب

أنا والدرويش

هَذَا البَحْرُ لَكَ
بَيَاضُهُ لَكَ
مَدُّهُ لَكَ
السُّكُونُ لَكَ
الهُدُوءُ وَالصَّمْتُ لَكَ
وَهَذَا الرَّمْلُ المُبَلَّلُ أَيْضاً
بِخُطَى القَادِمِينَ لَكَ.

أَمَّا الجَزْرُ
فَهُوَ لِي
لِيَ الصَّخَبُ
لِيَ الضَّجِيجُ
لِيَ الكَلَامُ العَنِيدُ
وَلِيَ أَيْضاً
الرَّمْلُ المُحْتَرِقُ
بِخُطَى الرَّاحِلِينَ
إِلَى البَعِيدِ.

هَادِئٌ بَحْرُكَ
وَبَحْرِيَ الهَادِرُ
يُعَارِكُ نَهَارَاتِي
أُجَالِسُهُ
يُبَادِلُنِي الوَجَعَ
أَتَّكِئُ عَلَى عَصَا ذَاكِرَتِكَ
أَهُشُّ بِهَا أَحْلَامِيَ المُتْعَبَةَ

Yusra al-Khatib

The Dervish and I

The sea is entirely
yours. Its pallor,
its ebb, its lull
are yours. Quiet is yours.
And this sand, wet
with the footsteps of those
who approach you.

As for the riptide,
it is mine.
The uproar is mine.
The clamor is.
Also my speech is obstinate,
also the sand is burning
with the footprints of refugees
fleeing.

Your sea is tranquil,
mine is battling
the day, raging.
I sit with it.
It gives me pain in return.
Throw me to the tide,
my recollections,
my exhausted dreams.

فَتُلْقِينِي عَلَى عَتَبَاتِ مَدِّكَ
عَلَى رَصِيفِ مِينَائِنَا المَهْجُور
أَسْتَرِقُ السَّمْعَ لِخَوَاءِ سُفُنِنَا
يَأْتِينِي صَوْتٌ
مَوْسَقْتَهُ ذَاتَ قَصِيدَةٍ
بِلَحْنِكَ وَجُنُونِكَ
هَذَا البَحْرُ لَكَ
وَكُلُّ الوَجَعِ لِيَ
بَيْنَ أَرْضِي وَبَحْرِكَ
تَتَفَتَّتُ قَصَائِدُنَا
تَتَسَرَّبُ طُفُولَتُنَا المُسْتَبَاحَةُ
كَرَمْلٍ مِنْ كَفّي القَدَرِ.

يُسَاجِلُ مَوْجُكَ حَنِينِي
فَتَقْرَأُ عَلَيَّ مَدَائِحَ بَحْرِكَ
ظِلَّكَ العَالِي
كَلَامَكَ العَابِرَ
جِدَارِيَّتَكَ
حَنِينَكَ لِأُمِّكَ
وَلَا شَيْءَ يُعْجِبُكَ
وَحِصَانُكَ
الَّذِي لَا يُشْبِهُ أَحَداً
لِمَاذَا تَرَكْتَهُ مِثْلِي وَحِيْداً؟

لَمْ يُلْقُوا
بِقَمِيْصِيَ المُدْمَى
عَلَى عَيْنَيْ أَبِي
لِيَعْرِفَنِيَ
وَأَسْتَدِلَ أَنَا عَلَيَّ
فَأَعُودُ لِقَصِيدَتِكَ بَصِيرَةً
وَأَسْرُدُ عَلَيْكَ
مِنْ قَصَصِ الأَوَّلِينَ

On the dock of our deserted port,
I eavesdrop on the hollow ships.
Is it a voice that rises, composing
melody and madness.
The sea is entirely yours.
This pain is entirely mine.
Between this land and this sea,
these lines disperse.
Our childhoods stream
like sand through open palms.

Your waves lap at my suffering.
You read your sea's panegyrics,
your shadow lengthening.
Your mural. I hear your
voice. You're calling
for your mother.
Why did you leave the horse alone?
Nothing pleases you anymore.
Why did you leave me
alone.

They did not throw
my blood-soaked shirt
before my father's eyes
for him to find me.
If he could find me
I would know where I am.
I return to the poem.
I still have my sight.
I will tell the stories
of our ancestors. Tomorrow

عَنْ غَد لَا يُشْبِهُ يَوْمَكَ
عَنْ حُلْمٍ لَا يُشْبِهُ أَمْسَكَ
وَحَاضِرٍ خَالٍ مِنْ وَجَعِ النَّايَاتِ.

لَرُبَّمَا يَكُونُ لَنَا
مِنْ اسْمِي نَصِيبٌ
وَأُسَجِّلُ مَرَّةً أُخْرَى
عَلَى بَوَّابَةِ الوَصِيدِ
سِيرَتَنَا الأُولَى
وَنُحَرِّرُ ذَاكِرَةً لِلْنِّسْيَانِ
لَعَلَّنَا نَنْسَى
حِصَارَنَا
وَعَصَافِيرَ لَكَ مَاتَتْ فِيْ الجَلِيلِ.

هل كُنْتُ مَعَكَ
أَوْ رُبَّمَا أَتَيْتُ بَعْدَكَ؟
أُوَقِّعُ أَدْنَاهُ
أُرِيدُ مَا تُرِيدُ
وَلَكِنْ يَا ابْنَ أُمِيَ
أَنْهَكَنِي الوُصُولُ
فَأَنَا مِثْلُكَ
لَا أبَ لِي
يُقَرِّبُنَا مِنْ البَعِيدِ
وَأَعُودُ
لِذَاتِ السُّؤَالِ العَنِيدِ
أَمَا آنَ لَهُ أَنْ يَنْتَهِيَ
هَذَا القَصِيدُ؟

غزة، ٢٠٢٣

will be unlike this day.
I will tell you my dream, it is
unlike yesterday's. And
today, by the city gates,
the reed flutes
have stopped wailing.

Perhaps we can share my name,
and begin our story
again at the city gates.
We free up memory,
we need it for forgetting.
Can we forget?
This siege.
These sparrows
that died in Galilee.

Was I with you then,
or did I come after?
I sign below
on the dotted line.
I want what you want.
My brother, I am so tired
of arrival.
And we have no father
to draw us closer
to our dreams.
Is it time then? Must the poems
end?

Gaza, 2023

ماهر المقوسي

في الريح

في الريح كان الليل يأخذ شكل حشرجةٍ ونايْ
بالناي كانوا يرسمون العمر أيكاً
والحنين وساوس الشطآن في جسد الغيابِ
وكلهم غابوا عميقاً
ثم جاءوا في صدايْ.
لا شيء يعدو في التلال سوى الظلالِ
وحين يكتمل السحاب يشدني برقٌ فأصرخُ:
أيها الضوء المباغت دلّني
من أين يأتي صوتها
هل من حفيف السرو يأتي
أم بهمسٍ من رؤايْ:
أنكون في همس الرمال كحاضرينِ
بقصتين عن الهوى والاغترابْ
وتدندن الريح الحكايا
للحبيب وللحبيبة مثلنا
كانا هنا ملء الدروبِ
يرتبان المفردات عن الأملْ
فيغيب في حُمّى الأحلام
كانا هنا ملء الجهات وإنما
كل الجهات تشابهت
وتقمص الحضنَ الخراب.

ومن الجهات تكاثُرُ الموتى
فكانوا يعبرون الظلَّ
ثم يسجلون حضورهم ما بين أنفاسي

Maher al-Maqousi

In the Wind

In the wind, night whistles and death-rattles,
lives quicken in thicketed groves,
waves whisper into lack's body.
All who disappeared into the deep,
resurface now, echo through me.
Nothing runs in the hills except shadows.
Clouds accumulate
and I am drawn to lightning:
sudden light, guide me
to the source of that sound—
cypresses rustling,
everything turning susurrant.
Will we still exist in the murmuring sand?
Will our stories of love and exile exist?
Now the wind hums two stories to us.
It says the lover and beloved
were here, they were everywhere,
preparing words about hope
that always dissipate into fever dreams.
They were here, they were everywhere.
But every direction is the same,
their embrace is carved in the ruins.

The dead multiply in every direction,
crossing through shadows

وأطلال النوايا . . .
كنت أهذي مثل طفلٍ
أدرك الوجع المخبأ في زوايا الاقترابِ،
وكلما يمّمت صوب الماء
تلسعني المرايا
كان صوت أبي يطل مبللاً بالضوءِ:
يا ولدي أتتك الريح
فاحمل كل جرحك والوصايا
واحترس من لدغة الإسفنج
سوف تفزعك المنايا.
من قلب جرحٍ غائرٍ في قلب زيتون البدايةِ
كان أصل طريقهم
مأوىً لأجراس الرحيل
من انتظار الليل فجراً في الصهيلِ
إلى اجترار الحلم صمتاً في الهديلْ:
قمرٌ بدا
غيمٌ شدا
حُفَّ المكانْ
بالأقحوانْ
كان النشيد فراشةً حطت على صدأ الكلامِ،
وكلما هب الرصاصُ
توزَّع المعنى شظاياً في الشظايا
قال ظل مسافرٍ:
يا ليتني ما كنتُ قد أسرفت في عدِّ الضحايا.

غزة، ٢٠٢٣

into my breath,
the debris of intention.
As a child, I was delirious,
seeing pain hidden in every corner.
Whenever I head to water,
mirrors sting me . . .
and my father's voice, drenched in light,
My son, the wind is rising,
carry your wounds. Carry your will.
Watch out for sea urchins.
Death will scare you.
From the pit of the deep wound
in the heart of the first olive,
the lovers' path starts.
From waiting at dawn for night, whinnying,
to chewing over a dream in silence, cooing—
a moon rises,
a cloud parts,
the place is surrounded
by chrysanthemums.
And song lands like a butterfly on rusted speech
as the bullets blow about.
Meaning splinters into shrapnel.
A traveler's shadow says—
I wish I hadn't counted the dead, the murdered.

Gaza, 2023

أمل أبو قمر

همهمات

تجذّرُنا الأرض في عمقها بضربة واحدة،
نأخذ كلنا الهوية نفسها،
ونستمد منها الحق في التفرغ بحرية دون ضرر.

في زاويةٍ ما
قطعة خاوية تعبث بها الريح جيداً، تأخذ تلة تطل على الفراغ، على كرسي أعوج سارقٍ متمرس
وأناس يصفقون للرذيلة . . .
في الأخرى . . .
بلادٌ كسرت عصاتها فوق كتفي،
وعلقت روحي على المشانق،

والأخرى
بلاد تكثر فيها مسارح العبث
وهمهمة الجائعين للحرية،
بلادٌ تشوهها أفواه تنبح بالوهم والكذب،
فيصفق جمهور مغفل . . .

في أضعف نقطة وأوهنها
يموت الكثيرون بلا رحمة . . .
يحتضرون جوعاً وخوفاً وبرداً،
ويطلقون حشرجتهم الأخيرة
ملتفين حول أنفسهم كأن هذه الآهة البعيدة هي نهاية هذا العالم.

غزة، ٢٠٢٣

Amal Abu Qamar

Murmuring

One bang and we're rooted deep in earth's bosom—
all grasping for the same self
from which we draw our rights—branch out. No harm, we
learn our dues, many forget.

In an empty corner of land, the wind gusts raising a hill overlooking an abyss.
A crooked chair, a seasoned thief, and
an audience is clapping,
whose staff breaks over my shoulders,
who hangs my soul in gallows?

Outside, the humming of those hungry for freedom.
Outside, the land deforms, mouths bark,
and the audience is still applauding.

At that empty corner,
famine, fear, cold.
Many are dying. Without pity.
They hold one another.
They hear their rattling hail the end of this world.

Gaza, 2023

آلاء القطراوي

كنت حزينة

أحزن إذا انفرطت إسوارة الخرز اللازوردي، وأبكي إذا ما تمزقت أطراف لعبة قديمة أخبئها سراً في خزانتي، أو إذا اتسخ بياض إحدى ملابسي، ولم أستطع إعادة لونه القديم، ومرة بكيت كثيراً حين مس رذاذ الكلور ثيابي، فصارت تشبه شبحاً معلقاً على حبل الغسيل، بكيت مراراً على صور تلاشت من هاتفي المحمول، وبكيت مرة حين ضاع مني كتاب ألف ليلة وليلة الذي وهبته لي صديقة في أمسية شعرية في غزة.

صديقتي الشهيدة هبة أبو ندى المعجونة بالمسك والعنبر، بكت ورداً على خدها المصقول بالملح، تتبع ظلي معي كالأنبياء، تقول لي: لا أحب ضياع الأشياء التي أحبها، فكل شيء يضيع وخز في الذاكرة.

أحياناً أحزن وأنا أنصت لأم كلثوم، ومن هواءٍ يعبر فجأة من شقٍّ مفتوحٍ في النافذة فيلفح قلبي، وأحزنُ إذا رأيتُ صورةً معلقة وقد مالت وكساها الغبار، وأحزن من ذبول الشغف في العيون الجميلة، ومن صراخ أبٍ على أولاده، وأغرق في الحزن إذا مررت على بائعة النعناع في آخر النهار وما زالت الشتلات أمامها لم تنفد.

ويجرح قلبي بكاء سائق غارق في سؤال الحياة والأقساط الجامعية لأبنائه الواقفين على سلم مائل وسط العاصفة. وأحزنُ إذا رأيتُ غريبا يتناول الطعام وحيداً، أو إذا رأيتُ عجوزاً يتوسّد طرف الطريق.

كان لديّ حزن خفيف، فضفاض، متفرّق كشظايا القنابل الغبية، وأصبحَ الآن لديّ حزنٌ واحد ثقيل قديم أبديّ، حزني على إخوةٍ آثروا محونا، و أغمضوا عيونهم عن دمنا الحرّ الساخن الذي تحمله الملائكة كل دقيقة، وتُسبّح قطراته الله ليل نهار.

غزة، ٢٠٢٤

Ala'a al-Qatrawi

I was sad

I was sad when my lapis bracelet broke, when the fabric of my old doll tore, when my bleach-spoiled clothes hung like ghosts on the line. Memories vanished from my cell, and I cried. At one Gaza poetry evening, I lost the *Arabian Nights,* gifted by my friend.

My friend, the martyr, Hiba Abu Nada. Formed from peaches and musk, crying roses on her salt-polished cheeks, following my shadow like a prophet, saying, "What's lost still pricks at your memory." And I remember what I've lost.

Listening to Umm Kulthum or music bereft of lyrics, I was sad. When air passed through a crack in the window, I was sad. When the picture on the wall was tilted and dusty. When I saw passion wither in a woman's eye. When a father shouted at his child on the street. And when I passed by the vendor at night, bunches of mint still lined up in front of her. I was sad.

My heart was wounded. By a driver crying over the question of life and school fees. By his children, as if they stood on an unsteady ladder amid a storm. By a stranger eating alone. By an old man lying down on the sidewalk.

Faint and shameful, blurred and mild, light sorrows, loose, dispersed like shrapnel before this bright extermination. Now I have one ancient heavy grief, undying. O brothers, you would wipe us out, turn a blind eye to this hot, free-flowing blood that's conveyed by angels who day and night glorify God.

Gaza, 2024

خيمة في السماء

ترى كيف تبدو لكم خيمتي
في السماء؟
وكيف ترونَ هديلَ الحمائمِ فوق
الزهورِ الهزيلةِ من دونِ ماء؟
وكيف ترون دموعي التي نبتتْ
نخلةً في دم الشهداء؟
وكيفَ تَرَوْنَ اشتياقي
الذي يُوقِدُ النارَ تحتَ القدورِ
فإنّي اكتشفتُ حريقاً بصدري
سيكفي على الأرضِ كلَّ النساء.

تُرى كيف تبدو لكم أمكمْ في السماءِ وكيفَ تَرَوْنَ حنيني المباح؟
وهل تعلمونَ بأنّي ألاحقكمْ في غناءِ العصافيرِ كلَّ صباح
وبينَ صراخِ الصغارِ إذا باغتونا
وطَوّقَنا الاجتياح
فأسألُ في خَجَلِ الأمهاتِ
تُرى أوجعوكم قبيلَ الرحيل الأخيرِ؟
وهل كانَ سهلاً عبورُ شهيدٍ ترجّلَ
يمشي بلا قلقٍ فوقَ نصلِ الرماح
فأسمعُ كركرةً للذينَ احتفَوْا بانتصارٍ عظيمٍ
فقدْ سبقونا لرؤيتهِ بينما نحنُ
نغرقُ في دمنا المستباح.

تُرى كيف يبدو لكمْ بحرُ غزةَ حين اشتهى
قبلةً بينما لم يجد أثراً للشفاه!
وحينَ تألّمَ شاطئهُ من دَمٍ عَالقٍ في جلودِ الحفاة!
وحينَ بكى مَنْ غَدَوا
صورةً مشتهاة!

A Tent from the Sky

What does my tent look like to you now
from the sky?
How do these cooing pigeons appear above
the parched flowers?
My tears—how do they look to you
sprouting palm trees from your martyr's blood?
What about my longing,
striking this fire beneath the pots?
Enough for all the women of this earth.

What does your mother look like to you now from the sky and how
do you see her longing?
You know I chase you in the sparrow-songs every morning?
And in shouts of children when they surprise me,
surrounded by the invasion.
I ask, with a mother's fear,
Did they hurt you right before your departure?
Was it easy to cross over then, as a martyr, dismounting, stepping
lightly over the spear tips?
I hear giggling—celebrations—a great victory.
We choke in our blood here, blameless.

What does Gaza's sea look like when it craves
a kiss and there's no trace of lips.
When its shore pains from the blood-sticky soles of the barefooted.
When those who became craved-after images, cried.
I wonder, Does our sea look just like us to you?
Is it its weeping that gathers into a wave, and exposes it.

تُرَى بحرنا مثلنا ربُّنا منذ بدءِ الزمان اصطفاه؟
يجاهدُ أحزانهُ
ثمَّ تفضحهُ موجةٌ صرخت من بكاه!

تُرَى كيف يبدو لكم شكل غزّةَ هل تعرفونَ
مدى مقلتيها؟
وهل فيهما أثرٌ للفراشةِ أم ماتَ مَنْ ينقشونَ بحنّائهمْ في يديها؟
وهل تسمعونَ صراخَ البيوتِ التي وقعتْ فجأةً
فوق أصحابها!
وهل تعرفونَ بأنَ حجارتها جرحتني
وأنّ الركامَ يئنُّ بصدري . . . وأنّي قُتِلْتُ مراراً بها . . .

تُرى كيفَ تبدو لكم أمّكم حينما تفتحونَ نوافذكم في السماءِ؟
لتُبصرَ نزفاً تعالى

دعوني أراها
ولو مرّةً واحدة
فقدْ يَبِسَ القلبُ في نصفِ آذارَ
ما عادَ ينمو بهِ شَجَرٌ للحمامِ
فأعطوا شفاهي لها
كي تُقبّلها . . .
ولوْ قُبلةً باردة!

وأعطوا لها رئتي
ربّما اختنقتْ دونها
ربّما ما استطاعتْ مناداةَ اسمي
فكان الركامُ ثقيلاً عليها
وكنتُ أحسُّ بها
فإني ورثتُ دماً
فيهِ حزنٌ قديمٌ/وسُمٌّ عتيقٌ/وذَبْحٌ سقيمٌ
وسرٌّ يعتّقهُ آل بيت النبيِّ
على سبحتي الزّاهدة.

What does Gaza look like to you now?
What does she look like?
Do you know the range of her vision?
Do you see the track of a butterfly in her iris?
Were the women who painted henna on her hands killed?
Do you hear the houses scream?
Do you hear them collapse over their people?
Do you know their rubble wounded me?
It groans in my chest. I was
killed. Over and over.

Did you open your windows in the sky
to see your mother bleeding?
Will you see her in the next body?
I saw a hand place pearls on her eyes
and, with a crescent moon, arch her eyelashes
back into their orbits so the night shone.
Then I gagged with longing.
You say, "We are as close as kohl to you.
Don't be sad. Every time tears fall
from your eyes, they fall from the sky."

Let me see Orchida
one more time.
The heart hardens in mid-March.
Trees don't grow anymore for doves.
Give my lips to her
to kiss . . . even a cold kiss, even once.

And give my lungs to her.
Without them, maybe she suffocated.
Maybe she couldn't call my name.
The rubble would have been too heavy for her.

وأعطوا لها شَعْرَ رأسي الطويلَ
أحبُّ أصابعها حين تلمسهُ
وتقولُ:
سأكبرُ حيناً
ويصبحُ شعريَ أطولَ منكِ
فقصّوا شعري لها
لكي لا تموتَ حبيبةُ عمري
بشَعْرٍ قصيرٍ
وأُمنيةٍ ناهدة!

دعوني أراها
لأخبرها أنّ شوقي لها ليسَ سهلاً
وأنَّ الخناجرَ أهونُ في طعنها
من جنونِ الغيابِ
وأنَّ عيونيَ في حزنِها الملحميِّ
طبولُ زنوجٍ
ضمورُ جبالٍ
زئيرُ سهولٍ
بكاءُ أسودٍ
عواءُ تلالٍ
صهيلُ المجرّاتِ
في دمعتي الماردة.

دعوني أرى وجهَ أوركيدتي
فقطْ
مرّةً واحدةْ!
دعوني أُقبّلها
ولو قُبلةً باردة!

غزة، ٢٠٢٤

I inherited blood,
I inherited old grief, ancient poison, a morbid sacrifice,
I inherited a secret blessed
by the Prophet's family forever
on my ascetic tasbih.

Give her my long hair now.
I loved her fingers when she touched it
saying, "I will grow up
and my hair will be longer than yours."
Cut my hair for her
so my sweetheart
won't die with short hair
and a maidenly wish.

Let me see her.
To tell her my longing is not easy.
That daggers' stabbing is easier
than the madness of absence,
and my eyes
for this epic grief
are like African drumming,
mountains shrinking,
the roar of plains, howling hills,
the snarl of lions,
braying of galaxies
all in my jinn-like teardrop.

Let me see the face of my little orchid
if even only once.
Let me kiss her.
Even one cold kiss.

Gaza, 2024

مريم قوش

الجاذبية

المهم أنني أشعر بعطشٍ شديد! وكوب الماء ها هو أمامي! ولكنني لا أستطيع شرب الماء الممزوج بالطين!
أجل! لا أستسيغ ذلك، يقول لي أخي محاولاً إقناعي: أنا تركتُ الماء ساعةً؛ فترسّب الطين في قاع الكأس ثم شربت! ولم أجد طعم الطين، جربي!
وضعت الكوب أمامي، وأخذت أتأمّل نزف الطين الذي يرشح في القاع ببطء مثل تاريخ قديم! تماماً مثل ساعة التاريخ الرملية التي ننتظر أن تنتهي، في هذا الطين بقايا أمم مضت، بقايا أجساد كانت لها حياة وذكريات، بقايا بيوت أصبحت ركاماً، بها بقايا ذاكرة كانت ستصبح حُبّاً لو أنها لم تُقتل!

مرت ساعة. مرت ساعتان . . . وأنا أتفرّج على الطين الذي يترسّب بالقاع، مساء أمس! ذهب أخي إلى الشيخ ليسأله عن صحة وضوئنا بماء ملطّخ بالطين، فابتسم الشيخ، وملأ وعاء الماء وتوضأ وقال له: صلّ معي! والآن يقول لي أخي الجملة ذاتها: ها أنا شربت فاشربي معي!

أنا لا أريد ولو متّ من الظمأ!
هل يجوز لي شرب الماء المتسخ بالتاريخ؟ هل يجوز لي شرب ذاكرة الأرض؟
يحدّق بي أخي، وبكأسه المملوء بالعتب يقول لي: كلنا شربنا منه!
فأجبته بحسرة: أنا اكتفيت! شربت تاريخي!

غزة، ٢٠٢٤

Maryam Qawwash

Gravitation

I'm really very thirsty. And there's a glass of water here. But I can't drink water mixed with mud. I can't. My brother says, "I left it an hour for the muck to settle and then drank. Didn't even taste clay. Try."

I place the glass before me—watch sludge hemorrhage and leach down—like old history, like an hourglass—we've been waiting for the end—through it, the remains of nations, the remains of bodies pass—they lived once, they had memories—the rubble of houses, the murdered recollections that would've grown into love.

One hour goes by, two—I watch mud lump at the base. My brother went to the sheikh to ask if we can wash in muddy water. If it's okay. The sheikh smiled, filled a bucket and gestured—pray with me. My brother says, "I drink this. Drink it with me."

No. I would rather not. Even if I die of thirst.
Can I drink water polluted with history? Can I drink the earth's memory?
My brother stares into me holding his cupful, saying, "We all drank."
I reply, "I have had enough. I already drank my history."

Gaza, 2024

هل نلتقي؟

هل نلتقي لو أن هذي الحرب يوماً تنتهي؟
هل نلتقي في شارع المختارِ، في حيّ الرمال أو الكرامة
هل نلتقي، في دهشة الكورنيشِ نرشف شاينا والفستقُ الحلبيُّ
يروي ما تبقّى من قشيبِ الغيمِ شوقاً اليمام.

هل نلتقي لو تنتهي
هذي الحروبُ في ذلك المقهى العتيقْ
نطل نحو كنيسةٍ ألقت على كاتب ولايةَ
شالها،
ونعود
نحملُ كل أسرارِ البنفسجِ للمخيمِ.

إننا عدنا
كأنا لم نغادرْ لحظةً
هل نلتقي؟ أم أن لقيانا خيال
الماء
في وجع البريقْ
وإذا التقينا هل نلاقي ذكرياتِ الروح في وجع المكان.

غزة، ٢٠٢٤

Will We Meet?

If this war ever ends, will we meet?
Shall we meet on al-Mukhtar Street? In al-Rimal or al-Karama?
Shall we meet on the charming Corniche, snacking on pistachios from Aleppo,
    sipping black tea,
quenching the fresh clouds, longing for doves.

Will we meet if these wars ever end?
Meet in that ancient café?
There, we will look toward the church—it throws a shawl to the state clerk.
Then we return,
carrying the violet's mysteries back to the camp.

And now we are back. As if we never left.
And if we meet, will we run into the memories of our souls?
Shall we meet? Or was that the illusion of the iridescent ocean—

Gaza, 2024

ناصر رباح

ساحة من رماد

الآن والأخبار غاضبة، وقلبي شاحب ودمي غبار،
الآن، لا بيت يدل شارعنا على سكانه، لا شارع يدل مدينة بأكملها على النسيان، كيف محا الطريق خطى المساء مشت عليه، وكيف تنكّر الدوري فجأة لشرفتنا الصغيرة؟
فلا سيارة المشفى أوصلت دمنا، ولا نحن جوعى، وأكملنا قبيل النوم وجبة الحطام.
القلب ساحة من رماد، يتوافده الحفارون صباح مساء، ينبشون قبور أصحابي القدامى، ويسرقون لي خشب الذكريات.

الآن والأخبار صاخبة، ويدي مدى، ودمي نهار.
الآن، والتاريخ عادتُنا، سنفتح باب قلعتنا لطاعون التتار،
والتاريخ لعبتُنا، هي خيمة أولى فقط وتكاثرت، وكأنها تعويذة الشعب الذي أحب هجرته كي لا يموت، كي يصل المدينة العنقاء في أحلامه، ويقيم هناك بيتاً من حطام سفينة نوح. والغار خيمتنا، وسراقة يمتطي دبابة، يفتش عن سوار النازحين.

لا شيء يغوينا إلا مهابة الإفلات من إطار المشهد العادي، هو أن نموت وأن نموت ولا نموت، لا شيء يغوينا سوى اكتراث الآخرين بموتنا وكأنه تفاحة، نصفها ليست لنا، ونصفها للريح.
يا غزة الملعونة المحبوبة المجنونة المقهورة المنبوذة المفتونة المنسية المذكورة ألف مرة في كتاب الحرب،
لا أنتِ ربة الموتى ولا كتابك اسمه حزن البلاد.

غزة، ٢٠٢٤

Nasser Rabah

A Battlefield of Ashes

As of now, the news is enraged, my heart is pale, my blood is dust.
As of now, no house guides my road to its residents, no road guides the entire city
to its oblivion, how has the street erased the footsteps of dusk? How has the sparrow
suddenly neglected our little balcony?
The ambulance has not delivered our blood nor are we hungry. Before bedtime, we
finished our meal of rubble.
The heart is a battlefield of ashes visited by gravediggers morning and night, they dig
up my friends' graves, steal for me the timber of their memories.

As of now, the news is loud, my palms are broad, my blood is daylight.
As of now, history is our habit, we open our citadel to the Tatars' plague,
history is only our first tent that multiplies, history is our game, the people's talisman,
for those who love their migration, for survival's sake. To reach the phoenix city in
their dreams. To build their house from the rubble of Noah's ark. The laurel tree's
our tent. Suraqa Ibn Malik rides a tank, searching for the refugees' bracelet.

Nothing enchants us except escaping the frame of our daily scene, to die, to die, to die,
and not to die.
Nothing enchants us, except others' sympathy for our death, as if it were an apple—half
of it is not ours, the other half is the wind's.
O damned, beloved, insane Gaza, O wretched Gaza, O pariah, forgotten, inscribed in
the book of war a thousand times—
you are not the goddess of death nor is your book called *Land of Grief.*

Gaza, 2024

المشفى بعيدة

كيف أسامحني وأنا تركتك في الزحام؟ السماء تمطر حديداً، والأرض مثل سجادة قديمة ينفض عنها الغبار. في الزحام كانت المشفى بعيدة، والسماء تواصل هذيانها، ذهب الأزرق والأخضر ولم يبق في عيني غير الرماد، والزحام يخرج الشارع عن رزانته فيسكر، وينوح: أنا غابة الموتى. عاد الشحاذون إليه، فوجدوه ضريراً، وأنا عدت لأبحث عن عيوني، فلم أجدها. كيف أسامحني، والمشفى بعيدة؟ عاد البكاء إلى بيته فلم يجده، عاد إلى ليله فلم يجده، وجاءني، شربنا نهاراً آخر، وبلاداً كثيرة، وقلنا: يا ذكريات كوني جميلة، فلم تكن، قلنا للشبابيك لا تجرحي عصافير القصائد، كانت البيوت جريحة، مدينة تفتش عن نفسها في الزحام، وأنا أجالس موتها، وكانت المشفى بعيدة.

غزة، ٢٠٢٤

The Hospital Is Far Away

How could I forgive myself if I left you alone in the crowd. The sky rains down iron and the earth's an old carpet getting shaken out. From the crowd, the hospital is far, the sky persists in its deliriums, blue and green are gone, and there's only ashes in my eyes. The crowd deranges the road. It grows intoxicated, muttering *I am the forest of the dead.* The beggars returned to the street and it was blind. *I went back to look for my eyes, but I couldn't find them.* How could I forgive myself and the hospital was far. The sound of crying returned but the street was not at home. It returned to this night but did not find her and then came to me. We drank another day, and there were so many countries, and we said: *Oh memories, be beautiful.* But they were not. We said to windows: *Do not injure poetry's sparrows.* Houses were badly wounded. A city searched for herself in the crowd, and I sat her down beside her death, and the hospital was far away.

Gaza, 2024

الطاعون

منذ عام لم أسمع أغنية في الشارع،
تقريباً لم يرقص أحد في حفلة عرس،
لم يأتِ باص المدرسة ولم يذهب،
وأحد لم يشتر وردة لأحد.
منذ عام نوزع كعكة الحرب الكريهة،
لم ننس طفلاً ولم ننس أي حديقة، لا كتاباً ولا أمنية.

في النهار نمرّن أعيننا السباحة في الدم، فلا تبتل،
وأن تخطئ في عد أطرافنا الناقصة،
نمرّنها في الليل كي تضيء الأسى،
وأن تشعل النار في خشب الانتظار.

منذ عام لم يحدث شيء،
ولم يكف عن الحدوث شيء.
تعال وافتح عينيك على آخرها أيها الموت:
نحن الضحية الأبدية المستحيلة،
تبكي بصمت نعم، وتصرخ حتى تشق ثوب السماء.
نحن الضحية التي جرحها مئذنة،
والتي دمها خلفها في الطريق إلى الجلجلة،
والتي غير كل الضحايا لا ترى قاتل أبنائها؛
لا تراه في الدموع،
لا تراه في القصيدة،
لا تراه . . .
لا تراه . . .
لا أحد يمكنه رؤية الطاعون.

غزة، ٢٠٢٤

Plague Song

I have not heard a street song for a year,
almost no one has danced at a wedding,
the school bus does not come and go,
and no one bought a rose for anyone.
For a year, we shared out vile war cake.
We didn't forget a child, a garden, a book, a wish.

During the day, we swim our eyes through blood without getting wet,
we miscount our missing limbs.
At night, we train our eyes to light the sorrow,
set fire to the woods of waiting.

For a year, nothing happens,
and nothing stops from happening.
Come, open your eyes wide, Death, and still wider:
we are undying, impossible victims.
Yes, a woman sobs, screams, tears the sky's gown.

We are that victim whose wound is a minaret,
whose blood trails behind her on the road to Calvary,
who, unlike others, does not see her children's killer,
she does not see him in tears,
she does not see him in poems,
she does not see him,
she does not see him.
Nobody can see the plague.

Gaza, 2024

مطر الليل

مطر الليل الحزين
فرقة موسيقى كاملة فقدت آلات العزف، وجاءت تبكي.

مطر الليل المتكاسل
ماكينة خياطة كبيرة وسوداء على مهل تخيط جراحنا.

مطر الليل الحافي
لم يجد في النهار من يحمله، فجاء متأخراً، ماشياً وبطيئاً.

مطر الليل العطشان
البلدة نائمة، طرق الأبواب كلها، لم يُفتح له بابٌ،
لم يكن أحد هناك، والشبابيك مطلية بالدموع.

مطر الليل الطويل
من يتنهد خلف الباب؟ من يتقلّب في سرير الفراق؟ بيدٍ مبتلة يقلّب في دفتر ماضيه اليابس؟
من يطلق على قلبه رصاص اليأس؟ من يتسلّق صرخاته الصامتة؟

مطر الليل البارد
لا نار في المدفأة، لا مدفأة في البيت، لا بيت في الشارع، فقط كانت الحرب تهرول عارية في المدينة العارية.

مطر الليل الصامت
وحده يصل الحديقة . . . وحدها تنتظر الأم . . . وحده يعود المحارب . . . وحده يكتب الشاعر . . .
وحده يموت البيت.

Night Rain

Rain on a sorrowful night.
The orchestra loses its instruments, comes wailing instead.

An idle night's rain.
A colossal black sewing machine stitching our wounds, patiently.

The night of unshod rain.
No one to carry it through the day, rain arrived late on foot and trudging.

Rain on a night of thirst.
The town is asleep. The rain knocks at every door. No one opens. No one is there.

Rain of the long night.
Who is sighing behind the door? Who tosses in the bed of separation? The rain turns the page of its arid past with wet hands. Who fires into its heart bullets of despair? Who climbs its cries?

A cold night's rain.
No fire in the fireplace, no fireplace in the house, no house, only war running naked through naked streets.

Rain on a quiet night.
Arrives alone into the garden. The mother waits alone. The warrior returns alone. The poet writes alone. The house dies alone.

مطر الليل المتأخر
يسقي البيت المهدوم ويسقي المقبرة، وينسى أن الأحد الميت كان يفكر في الأثنين، وكان السبت يهرول نحوهما لكن لم يحدث، حيث أمطرتهم الطائرات نهار الجمعة، وانتهى كل شيء.

غزة، ٢٠٢٤

Rain late at night,
watering the ruins, watering the graves. Rain forgets the dead. Sunday ponders Monday, Saturday runs toward them, doesn't make it. On Friday fighter planes rain down on them and it is over.

Gaza, 2024

لا شيء يقتلني، لا شيء

أموت ببطء يا ريتسوس،
ببطء أكثر يا ناظم حكمت
يمرُ بي سجناء قدامى، يقولون: هل تذكرتنا؟
فأعرف حينها من أكون،
سجنٌ فارغ، يلوح لي ميتون عابرون،
فأدعوهم لمتحف الذكريات،
غير أن . . .
لا شيء يقتلني، لا شيء.

أموت ببطء يا لوركا،
ببطء أكثر يا نَوَّاب
حطبٌ يتأملُ ذاتَه، جوار مدفأة مطفأة،
عجوزٌ يفقد أسنانه، يود الغناء، فترتبك المعاني.
شارع يخسر كل يوم باباً ونافذة،
وتعبرُ السماء طائرات.
غير أن . . .
لا شيء يقتلني، لا شيء.

أموت ببطء يا ناصر رباح،
ببطء أكثر يا نيرودا
مليوني مسيح هنا، يصعدون إلى الله حفاة عراة،
بالطناجر الفارغة يزعجون روما النائمة،
يلقون أسماء أطفالهم في الهواء،
فتمطر السماء أغنيات.
غير أن . . .
لا شيء يقتلني، لا شيء . . .
أنا حجر زاوية المكان.

غزة، ٢٠٢٤

Nothing Kills Me, Nothing

I die slowly, oh Yiannis Ritsos,
Even slower, oh Nazim Hikmet.
From ancient times, the prisoners pass by asking, *Do you remember?*
Then I know who I am.
Empty prison, the dead pass by, waving to me.
I invite them into my museum of memory
Yet nothing kills me, nothing.

I die slowly, oh Federico García Lorca,
Even slower, oh Muthaffar al-Nawab.
The timber contemplates itself in the extinguished fireplace.
A toothless old man starts to sing, but his words jumble.
Daily, a street loses a door, a window.
Airplanes pass by overhead.
Yet nothing kills me, nothing.

I die slowly, oh Nasser Rabah,
Even slower, oh Pablo Neruda.
Two million messiahs ascend to God, barefoot and naked,
Holding out empty cooking pots, perturbing Rome's sleep.
They toss their children's names into the sky,
Until it is raining down song
On me, the keystone, touchstone, taproot of this place.
Yet nothing kills me, nothing.

Gaza, 2024

شجاع الصفدي

العالم يصدأ

العالمُ يصدأ
مثل تروسِ الساعةِ
مثل القلب.
قلت ساعتان من الانتظار تكفي
هجرتُ المحطة، وفي الطريق للرجوعِ كنت أعدُّ خطاي
لطالما في العمرِ خانتني الأرقام.
سنة، خمسة، عشرة، لم أسجّل تاريخاً، لم أحتفظ بذكرى.
قالت: ما جدوى الذكريات في عالمٍ من صدأ؟

العالم يصدأُ مثلَ حنينٍ كاذب، قلوبُ النساء تصدأ كذلك،
مثل أوتار الكمنجات حين تهجرها الموسيقى،
قلوب الرجال ذات صريرٍ عالٍ حين تُهجَر،
كنتُ حُبلى بالأمنيات،
أنجبتُ لك الخرافةَ، وقطفتَ مني شهوةَ المعنى،
أهديتَني ساعةً، لم تهدِني الوقت، أهديتني حبيباً، ولم تهدِني الحب.

وشمتكَ على كتفي أثراً أبدياً يدلّكَ عليّ ورحلت.
نسيتُ الضوءَ مشتعلاً في غرفةِ الأبدِ، لم أكن أدرك أن السيدةَ اللطيفة التي تقترب
تسعى للانتحار.
كانت الفراشةُ فدائياً يائساً، لم ينسَ الأسى، فاحترق.

صار رمادها لعنةَ العمرِ، نسيتُ المدنَ التي صنعتُ فيها الذكريات
نسيتُ هزائمي، جحودي، نسيتُ الطريق إلى محطة الانتظار، نسيتُ خطاي.
إلا وجهكِ يا حبيبتي كان جميلاً، قاسياً، فنسيتُ أن أنساه.

Shuja'a al-Safadi

The World Is Rusting

The world is rusting
like the gears of a clock.
I leave the waiting station, counting my steps.
I say *To wait two hours is fine,* but
numbers always betray me. A year, five,
ten. Who can store away history now? Who can keep their memories?

The world rusts into its false nostalgia. The heart too.
Like violin strings just as the music breaks from them, our hearts
also echo.
I have a watch,
but no time.
I have a compass
tattooed on my shoulder,
but I left the light on in the eternity room.

I did not know that the woman tenderly approaching was suiciding—
a butterfly, a guerrilla, a fighter, and decided. She never forgot her resentment.
She burned. Her ashes, a curse to life.

Now I am oblivious to this city, oblivious to my defeat, to my wandering
to the waiting station, to my own steps.
Her face. Soon I must remember to forget it.

لم يكن دمعاً.
لم يكن دمعاً، كان خيبة أمل،
وكنتُ مزيجاً من حجرٍ ونار.

غزة، ٢٠٢١

But it wasn't tears.
It wasn't tears. It was disappointment.
And now I am become an amalgam of stone and fire.

Gaza, 2021

أنا الكومبارس في نصّك!

تعالَ نبني علاقة هشّة
نكتبُ قصةً مثلاً؟
أو نرفعُ سقفَ الأمنيات على أعمدةِ المخيّلة
هذا بيتنا، في الركن جيتارٌ ومزهرية
هناك مقعدان لنشرب قهوتنا معاً
هنا نتابع التلفاز، نشرةُ الأخبار عاريةٌ مثلي من الحقائق المجرّدة.

يروقني التحديقُ في انتباهِكَ
شغفكَ بالسياسةِ وأخبار الحرب
وأخفي سخطي من انشغالكَ عنّي
أنا الحياةُ، وأنت منشغلُ بالموت!
حسناً، سأكملُ ما بدأت:
على الحائطِ لوحةٌ لدافنشي،
في الجهةِ المقابلة رفوفُ المكتبة
أزيّنها بصورةٍ لي
لي وحدي.

أخشى أن أضع صورتَنا معاً
فتهملُها كما أهملتَ قلبي
صورتي وحدي ذكرى مؤجلة
تضعُ احتمالاً أنك لن تنساني.
أنا الكومبارس المُذعِنُ في نَصِّكَ،
كلّما تعرضتَ لجرحٍ في أغنية،
أو احتضنتكَ غابة.
طلبتَ مني أن أطعمَ الطيرَ من جسدي
ووقفتَ تدقُّ الطبولَ على رأسي،
تلك كانت طقوسُكَ في الكتابة.

The Author's Psyche Addresses His Persona

However fragile, let's make a pact,
let's make up a story,
let's raise the ceiling of our wishes
on pillars of imagination.
Let's make our house—in the corner: a guitar, a vase,
two chairs. Let's drink coffee,
watch TV. The news is, like me, stripped of facts.

I like staring into your attention,
scanning politics, scanning war.
You're up to your ears in it.
I hide in my life. I hide in my disdain.
You are busy with death.
I am finishing what I'm beginning.
Hanging on the wall—da Vinci—
and opposite, all the library's shelves, full,
and a photo of me. Just me.

I presume you won't forget me. It is still possible.
I'm a yes-man, an extra in your script.
Whenever you came across a wound in a song,
whenever you were held by a forest,
whenever you asked me to feed my flesh to the birds,
you stood there. Absentmindedly drumming my head.
These were your writing rituals.

علاقتنا هشّةٌ جداً
مثل قصابٍ وأضحية
أنت تكتبُ بعرقي المالح
بينما أجوب الزوايا عاريةً
وأخفي هلعي
مثل فريسةٍ احتياطية تنتظر الخاتمة.

غزة، ٢٠٢٤

Our bond is so fragile,
a butcher and his victim.
You write with my briny sweat.
I roam the room's corners naked,
I hide my panic—
waiting for its end, a prey on standby.

Gaza, 2024

خالد شاهين

عندما يُسقط الله مطراً وتغرق الأرض

حين يسقط الله مطراً وتغرق الأرض من أجل زهرة، هو الحبُ الذي لا يعرف عنه أحد. أما بعد:

المدنُ كما النساء تحفظُ أسماء فاتحيها، ألمح ضوءً وسماءً رعدت، تهيأت لصورة جديدةٍ وأسئلة، أعرفُ أنّ الله هو المُصوّر وعنده علم الأجوبة. فلماذا غزة لا تتزوج عند أخواتها، أريحا، القدس، جنين؟

تسكن بجوار الخليل، لماذا بعيدةٌ، حزينةٌ، وحدها في الصحراء تقف أمام البحر؟ ما الفرق بينها وبينك، «كلانا يلهث» أنتَ إلى ناي وهي إلى ضالتك،

السّروةُ عجوزٌ ترقص في عرسِ حفيدِ حفيدتها! النخلة صبية تلوح «وين ع رام الله»، بلادي شجرة برتقال تحرس ممرات الغابةِ العارية. المساءُ جبال تجدل منحدرات، مدن تصبغ الهواء بلونِ الطين. غزة: بلادٌ تسهرُ مع قاتليها، تهادن ليلاً ضحاياها، جبهتها خضراء وقد زينت اسم الله لتنجو من حفلةٍ تنكريه.

أسأل نصفي الأول كيف تحوّلت أنت عضوياً؟ لي عشر أمهات، وولدتُ يتيماً من روحِ امرأةٍ صامت عن الشهوات، وتَزَوجت من سياج أرض يابسة، من صبّك في اللوز وأخذ النطفة نحو الزهر؟

كيف تكوّنت! أنتَ ليلةَ حبٍ أعدّها الله لأمّك، عنقوداً تعلّقَ في سماء الدالية، فراشةٌ أخطأت دربها في الحديقة فكنتَ أنت، النصف الأول من اسمي يجرّ حرفين معه إلى الدنيا، أسكن في بلادٍ لم يمسسها سوء، الطرق فيها أعرفُها من الصَبّار، ومن ليمونة حكّت رغبتي، من قبائل استضافت هجرتنا الأولى في مراعيها كـي نحرس خوفهم وتبيت نساؤنا في جرنِ قمحٍ، فمن قتل البحر الميت!

من سرق من المِلح الزُرقة! لا مكان نكون فيه غير هُنا كي تخضرّ الحقول، مرعبة يا أبي هجرتنا كالنوقِ إذا عبرت نهراً، والرصاص الذي مرّ من فوق رؤوسنا قال إن الحياة دقائق وثوان.

Khaled Shaheen

When God pours out rain and the earth floods

When God pours out rain and the earth floods for the sake of a flower, it is a love that no one knows. Afterward:

cities, like women, commit the names of those who raped them to memory. I glimpse a light and a thundering sky, I ready myself for a photo op and questions. I know God is omniscient. Why won't Gaza marry like her sisters, Jerusalem, Jericho, Jenin?

Gaza dwells beside Hebron, so why so distant, sad, alone in the desert, standing before the sea? What's the difference between you and her? We're both gasping. You, into a reed flute, she into what she's lost.

The cypress is an old woman dancing at her great-grandson's wedding. The palm tree is a girl waving *where are you headed to in Ramallah?* My home's an orange tree that guards the path through the bare woods. The dusk, a mountain range braiding its slope.

Cities paint the air the color of clay. Gaza must stay up late with her killers and placate the victims. Her forehead's green where she's emblazoned God's name, where she's tried to escape from a masquerade.

I ask my body's first part, how it was figured. *I have ten mothers. I was born an orphan to the soul of a woman. She refrained from desire, she married a barren land.*

بين الحب والحرب راء لإرباك

الرعشة ورعشة الماء ارتواء.

غزة، ٢٠١٤

Who molded you into the almond, transmitted seed toward the blossom? A bunch hanging in the grapevine-sky, a butterfly losing its way in the garden,

and so you came into being, your first name dragged its two letters into the world—

Now I dwell in a land once untouched by misfortune, a land whose alleys I know by the cactus, by the lemon tree, by the tribes who hosted us in their pastures on our first migration, so we would guard their fear, and our women dwelt in their mills.

Who killed the dead sea? Who stole blue from salt? We have nowhere to be but here so the fields turn green. Father,

our migration is harrowing, camels cross the river, bullets pass overhead.

And he says *Life is minutes and seconds.* The shivering of water quenches. It is sufficient.

Gaza, 2014

أنبحُ على ظلي وأحرسُ الهواء

نباحٌ أول.

مُخيلتي جروٌ صغيرٌ، كلما جاع ينبح، يلتهم الضجر. ضدي قد يصبح صديقي مع مرور الأزمنة، أَحبُ النساء لقلبي، الجدة، واللاتي يُجدن السطو على ما بين السطور. و من نظرة عين يعرفن ما يدور في المخيلة. من يوم الهجرة وأنا محبوسٌ كماءٍ تأخر في النزول من «الحنفية». خوفي يتراكم فوق كرسي متحرك. أُنصتُ للحزن بأزرارٍ مقطوعة. أبدو كنبيٍ تلاحقه الصبية بالطوب. كيف سأنجو وقد نزل الصحابة عن الجبل! كيف تُبررُ الهزيمة؟

من أطفأ نور الشمس من المغرب لقادر أن يستعيد عافيته لتلةٍ نائيةٍ في أقصى الشرق. ظلي شكلٌ آخر لي، كائن لا أعرفه وأكثر مني صار معروفاً في الظهور والمراوغة. ببراءةٍ سأنجو والنار تعلو المداخن. تموت الأرض بداء السل. تفاريح الأرغول مسموعة عند جارتنا مريم والنسوة يغنجن «مهاهات» مفهومة وتعطي أكثر من تفسير. أستمدُ عافيتي من سيدةٍ تبيع الفرح.

قالت لي: لمن تلكَ الرؤى؟

قلتُ: لكلبٍ على باب كهفٍ لم يدخله أحد. ولي.

أنبحُ على ظلي وأحرسُ الهواء.

غزة، ٢٠١٤

I bark at my shadow, I guard the air

My imagination is a puppy. Whenever she's hungry, she barks. She devours boredom.
My enemy may befriend me in time. The women dearest to me are grandmothers,

they read between the lines. From the look in your eyes, they see the images in your mind.
Since the day of migration, I've been frozen like water in a faucet, suspended.

My fear is piled into a wheelchair. I listen to grief with broken buttons. I look like a prophet
chased by boys grasping bricks.

How will I survive until the companions come down from the mountain? How do I justify
defeat? Whoever extinguishes the sun's light where it sets may restore it to a remote hill
in the far east.

My shadow is another form of me, a being I don't recognize, known to appear and evade.
He'll survive innocently while fire rises up the chimneys.

Meanwhile, the earth dies from tuberculosis, our neighbor Maryam listens to the reed pipe,
the women chant *mahahat,* with clear and manifold meanings, I'm restored by a woman
who spreads joy.

She asks, who are those visions for?

For a dog at the mouth of a cave that no one has entered.

It is me. I bark at my shadow. I guard the air.

Gaza, 2014

جبر غيث

حين يشتعل الموقد

يجرحك الرماد
حين لا يدقُّ أحد بابك
يشاركك دفء الموقد
وشاي الحطب
وتقول: لا بأس، لعل الأصحاب لديهم ما يشغلهم
ولكنك حين ينطفيء الموقد
ويصير آخر ما تبقى لديك من حطب رماداً
وتبات وحيداً كذئب ضيعه القطيع
تدرك لِمَ لم يدق بابك
من الأصحاب أحد.

غزة، ٢٠٢٢

Jabir Sha'ith

When the Hearth Burns

The ash harms you.
Nobody knocks on your door.
Nobody shares the hearth. Nobody shares your stove-warmed tea.
And you say *It's fine, it's fine, perhaps they're busy.*
Then the fire goes out.
Then the last logs are embers.
And you spend the night like a lone wolf.
And you know why nobody knocks.

Gaza, 2022

آثار سرب النمل

لم يبق في الركوة قهوة
والجمر في الموقد ترمد وذرته ريح جائرة
وحولي لا أرى إلا جندباً يحوم حول ما تبقى من رمق الجمر في الموقد
ونملة وحيدة تفتّش في رمل الخيمة عن فتات
وعما خطّه سرب النمل من أثر

غزة، ٢٠٢٢

Traces of the Swarm

No coffee left in the coffeepot.
Embers turning to ash, ash whirling up into the unruly wind.
Beside me, I see a locust hovering above
The stove. I see nothing else.
Then a lone ant searching the sand for crumbs,
Searching for what the swarms left behind.

Gaza, 2022

هاشم شلولة

قصة الدم يرويها المنصتون

دمنا يلوّن تاريخَ الأشياء؛
نحن الذين لم نكذِّب الحقيقةَ الوحيدة
بقصدٍ غير مقصودٍ مرّة.
أيّ ضياءٍ سيولد من هذه الحلكة الطويلة؟
أيّ مبلغ سيدفعه الزبائنُ لقاء الموت للمُلّاك؟

زراعةُ وردةٍ في نصف الصاروخ المتفجّرِ بعد انهيار البيت
صارت أمراً مضحكاً.
ليس لأنَّ الأسبابَ أغرقتها الدماء،
ولا لأنَّ عدَّاد الموتى في علوٍّ مستقيم ومرتب
بلَّ لأننا ننظر إلى الله مرّةً،
وإلى حواسنا مراراً . . .

كيف كانت الشعوب الحزينة؟
والقصد، كيف تكون عندما يطويها الخرس، وهي ترى منشارَ النهايةِ يقطِّعُ شجرَ الكلام المستغيثِ
بظُلمةٍ أولى . . . أولى فقط؟
ظلمةٍ غير التي تطول كهذا النزيف . . .

سأصنع الوهم وأنا أتعرّى كأسمائنا كلِّها/
سأصنعه عندما يتحول سمعي رغيفاً؛
أشد أزر قامتي به بعد عمرٍ من جوعٍ أليف.

صواريخُ،
صراخٌ
وصروح بالأرض تُوارى . . .

Hashem Shalola

Blood's Tale Narrated by Its Audience

The history of things is painted in our blood,
and we never deny the only truth
intentionally. Only perhaps once. Once unintentionally.
So what lights will be birthed from this long night,
what will settlers pay for the rightful owners' deaths?

Planting a rose in the exploded missile
after the house collapsed
became a laughing matter,
not because reasons are drowning in their blood,
or the death count is steady, or orderly, or tidy,
but because we look to God just once
and to our senses again and again.

How have these mournful people lived?
I mean, when they are folded into muteness, watching the saw of end-times
chop down the tree of speech, which cries out to the first night.
It is dark beyond this perpetual bleeding.

Perhaps I will create an illusion. Perhaps
I will undress until I'm naked as our names—
when my hearing turns into a loaf of bread,
when I stand up straight having tamed my lifelong hunger.

Missiles, screams, edifices leveled . . .
I'm haunted by the report of a disaster beginning with the letter *sād*.

لا يبارحني نبأٌ أفرغَتْه وقيعةٌ من حرف الصاد؛
كما لا يبارحني قلقُ الأزمنةِ كلِّها
مذ آدم حتى آخر سبتٍ حلّ.

سأصنع الوهم الآن، أو بعد ذلك ربما.
الوهم ليس قراراً . . . هل هناك قرار إذن؟
إن أوحد قرارٍ والأفحش والأوحش يا يوفتشينكو العزيز؛
هو الانتحار بتبيان الأسماء/
بتبايُنِها بين موت أصحابها أو جُرحِهم؛
كأن تذهب لتصلي أو تغني أو تريد . . .

تحضر عرساً للحقيقة البائدة؛
يتحول بعد دقيقتين لبركة دمٍ
يتزحلق فيها أهلُ العُرس كلُّهم . . .
يُكلّفك ذلك جنازةً بصدرِ الأغاني،
وليس العكس لو مرّة بساحل التاريخ المتعرّج . . . مرةً واحدة.
كل شيءٍ تُباصرُه اكتناهاتُ الخطيئة
حين تستعدُّ الحربُ لفهم أسباب الحياة
فيصعب الفهم عليها
فيُحسَم الجدلُ؛ ليسقُط بعد إذن سقفُ الأبد
يصيرُ كلُّ شيءٍ مؤقتاً
كأنّ الكلَّ وردةٌ في كأس.

الموت برسمِنا افتعالٌ لعبثٍ كبير؛
إذا كان ترقيمُ الأرواح عنواناً
إذا كانت الأشياءُ التي سوى الجسد سيدةً/
فهذا الجسد سهل كزلزالٍ يحدثُ سريعاً،
يهزُّ الأسماء والبصائر والنعوت . . .

I'm haunted by the anxiety of every age
from Adam to the last Sabbath.

Yes I will create the illusion now, or must I wait.
I can't decide. Is there *decision?*
The only decision, the obscenest decision, O dear Alexander Yuvchenko,
the most monstrous—
to suicide by naming names,
reporting dead bodies and the wounded
as if you were going to pray or sing or wanted to.

You attend the wedding of a dying truth.
But it turns into a bloodbath within two minutes.
The wedding guests all get murdered.
It costs you a funeral and a chest full of songs,
not the other way around along the crooked coast of history.
Once everything was seen through the eyes of sin
then war got ready to teach the causes of life
but it was hard to understand—
and isn't the debate already settled as, now, the ceiling of eternity collapses
and everyone becomes temporary
like a rose in a glass.

Death, from our perspective, is only a big absurdity.
As if the numbering of souls were just a label.
If only the things of this world did not contain my body,
if only they were a lover, if only this body of mine was quick
as an earthquake, shaking off names, visions, attributes.

تمضي طائرةٌ بعد ذلك؛ ليصير الخطاب للغبار
للدم/دمُنا لم يعُد عزيزاً،
وهو المُراد من حلمٍ أخير،
المُراق انصهاراً بألحانِ النزال المكسور المُهان . . .

نعلم أنّك تعرف غزة يا حبيبي،
تراها وتبتسم/
تراها وتغضب،
ونراها ونرجوك بإمارةٍ؛ يُتم عميق والبُكاء . . .
ونعلم أنَّ البُكاء حرفة الأسطورة نحن الذين فقدنا الأساطير،
واتضح الفقد، ويتضح مع كلِّ ليلٍ وصاروخ وموتٍ جديد . . .
نعلم أنَّ اللانهايةَ صوتُ حاجتنا للنهاية . . . فاحتوينا،
هذا رجاء الغرقى في الحجارة.
هذا رجاء الغرقى.

غزة، ٢٠٢٤

Just now a fighter jet passes overhead, speech is dispossessed by dust,
by blood—our blood which is no longer precious—
which is the point of this last dream
spilling into melody over our broken, humiliated struggle.

We know you know Gaza.
You see her and smile.
You see her and feel furious.
We see her and beg you with anguish and tears.
We know that crying is the craft of legends, and we have lost legends.
Loss comes into focus with every night, every missile, every death.
We know endlessness is the voice of our longing for ending—so embrace us.
Ours is the wish of those who are drowned,
ours is the wish of those who are drowned in stones.

Gaza, 2024

قصاصات منسية في حقيبة الحرب

دُفِن صوتي الخفيض
ضحكتي الساخرةُ من العالم
بلاغتي المُجهدةُ من الحَفْر في اللغة
صار كل سنتمتر أمشي فوقه قبراً.

⁂

أضئ قلبي مرّة أيها الجنديّ
مرّةً واحدة؛
لأنطق.

⁂

كان صمتي موسميّاً
عند اشتداد الفجر مثلاً
أو وقت امتزاج الملحمة بالأخرى
لكنّ بحراً فيَّ كان يقول:
عبثٌ مؤقت،
وسيتسلل الغبارُ إلى ما وراء حدود الحصار.

⁂

بداوتي أنيقة
تُلبِسُ الدم الفائرَ قصةَ يسوع آخر،
وتفكُّ أزراها كأنّها تستعدُّ لحميمية القاصِّ المفقود
تعبُّ الليل كالزنجبيل،
وتحتفي باليُتم.

Scraps of paper forgotten in the war bag

That voice—deep, buried—is mine.
That is my cynical laughter at the world.
My fluency's worn from digging into language.
Every centimeter I walk on is a grave.

Once, just once, Soldier, kindle my heart—
just once—
with speech.

My silence was seasonal—
when dawn broke
or one epic fused with another—
a sea inside me spoke:
brief senselessness, then
dust will snake far past the frontiers of this siege.

Being Bedouin is stylish,
clothing my ebullient blood.
This is the story of a different Christ,
unbuttoning his skin as if anticipating
intimacy with the lost narrator.
Swallowing the night like ginger tea.
Toasting orphanhood.

كنتُ دائمًا حذِراً من الأبد
خائفاً من يدٍ تغرقُ في رماد الخوابي
لكنّي الآن منبسطٌ
وثرثار . . .
هكذا تفتحُ المدافعُ قلبها لشاعرٍ غريب.

لي أحزانٌ كثيرة
أعمقُها نسياني شطيرتي في الفرن واحتراقُها . . .
أقمتُ مأتماً يومها،
كأنَّ بلاداً نُسيَت في حقائب المهاجرين.

الحرب نصفُ الكأس الممتلئ
الكأسُ مستريحٌ على الأصبع ومرتبِك
صاحب الأصبع يركض،
والشمس تهامسُ البحر
النهار يُهزَم
وقلبي طافحٌ بكينونة الماء المندلق من الكأس.

علاقتُنا بالنجاة غريبة
كظهر السكين بعنق الطائر
يُهيَّأ لنا نصلٌ،
وبعد عمرٍ فاشل
نلمِسُ زجاج المحطات المنفية.

قبل أن تلِد الحمامةُ
اكتُشفَ الخطأ،
ولم تضع بيضاً
تركت توقيعاً يقول:
لكلِّ قتيلٍ أجنحة.

I was always wary of eternity.
Wary of a hand sinking into the ashes of a waterpot.
But now I am awake and garrulous.
That's how the cannon opens its heart to a poet.

I have many sorrows.
Once to add insult to injury,
I forgot my sandwich on the grill, and it burned.
That day I held its funeral.
And a whole country disappeared into a migrant's abandoned bag.

War is a glass.
It rests against fingers, half-filled—
why is the body holding it running.
Why is the sun whispering to the sea.
Even the day has been defeated.
And my heart overflows and spills from its cup.

Our bond with survival is eccentric—
a knife's blunt edge on a bird's neck.
A blade that has been sharpened just for us
even before our failed lives began.
But still we touch the glass, at each station of exile.

Before the dove's eggs hatched
the mistake was discovered.
She didn't lay any eggs.
There was a note left behind:
All the murdered will grow wings.

ـ۰

ليلٌ واحد كلُّ الليالي
النهارات نهارٌ واحد
الأوقاتُ كذلك
لكنَّ اسمي جماعةٌ
فرَّقَتها مظلمةُ الخيام.

ـ۰

حملتُ حبري على كتفي
لأرسم التجربة وخلاصاً تأخّر
لكنّي اكتشفت انسكابَ الحبر على جسدي
بفعل الطريق ورجفة الخطوات
صارت التجربةُ أضغاث أحلام
لمن أراد الرسم.

ـ۰

كان تاريخي الصغير دزّينةَ حروبٍ؛
أردتُها حرباً واحدةً تصنعُ قصيدةً
أستجذبُ بها حرارةَ المُصفقين/
تجليّهم الحزين، ووقوفَهم عن الكراسي . . .
اكتشفتُ لاحقاً أنَّ القصةَ أكبر،
وأنَّ إنساناً صنعته حروبٌ كثيرة
مذابحُ أكثر ومشنقة . . .

ـ۰

دمٌ خالصٌ هذه المرة
غيرُ مختلطٍ ببارود الصواريخ
هو هذا الذي يسقطُ من عقولِ من لم تصبهم الغارات،
وهم يدركون بأبصارهم ما بعد التفجير
من حيزٍ مُعمّرٍ صار حسرةً
وحسرةً صارت حيِّزاً معمّراً.

Every night was one night.
Each day was one day.
Time was always the same,
but my name was a people
divided by the sabotage of tents.

I carried my ink on my shoulders
to sketch the experience of my delayed redemption
but ink spilled all over my body
with each trembling step I took on the road—
experience is vain, experience is a dream
for those who want to dream it.

My little history was a dozen wars.
If only they were one war and that war were a poem,
attracting passion, attracting applause—
now the audience is sad, now it stands up from its seats . . .
Later I'd learn the story is vast.
The human is molded from many wars,
and still more massacres, more executions.

Raw blood this time,
raw, without gunpowder,
flowing from the minds of those
who were spared air strikes.
They see the aftermath:
a lively place turned to regret.
But regret is a place, a place we can live in.

كلُّ حكايات الحرب الشهيدة
لا زالت يقظةً على سرير الحياة
تُكمِل سيرها البطيءِ نحو الخلود
إلّا نحن الذين لم نُمت؛
انتهينا منذ أول بابٍ فتحته يدُ أكتوبر الفظّة
أصبحت عظامنا لقمةً بفم تاريخٍ كان هنا
ربما؛ كان هنا
وربما كنّا . . .

تُقضى ديون فجرٍ تأخّر
يسقطُ طفلٌ كورقةٍ من تينة الحياة
ويسقطُ معه مطرٌ من قلب امرأةٍ/ساقية
تلك قصةُ خريفنا المذبوحِ ذبحةً
تمتد من النيل إلى الفرات.

جئنا من الصرخةِ
عشنا ألفِ سنةٍ بداخلها،
ولم نسأل من أيِّ حنجرة اندلقنا
فجأة؛ سكتَ كلّ شيء
ولم يعُد لصارخٍ حنجرة
قيل في الأثر أنَّ ملحمةً ذوّبت آثارنا.

غزة، ٢٠٢٤

All the war stories are martyred too,
still wide-eyed on the bed of life
pursuing a slow march into immortality.
Except for us who did not die,
but came to an end through that first gate swung open
by the harsh hand of October.
Our bones are morsels in the mouth of history. It was here,
was it not. It was here.
We were here.
Were we not.

The dawn's overdue debts are settled now,
a child falls from the fig tree of life like a leaf,
rain falls from a woman's heart—a waterwheel—
this is the story of how our slaughtered fall.
They fall from the Nile to the Euphrates.

We sprang from a scream.
We lived in it a thousand years.
We did not ask whose throat we rose from.
Then, all of a sudden, everything is silent,
the screaming has no throat.
It is said that an epic absorbed all trace of us.

Gaza, 2024

هلا الشروف

خذيني أيتها الأرض البعيدة

خذيني أيّتُها الأرضُ البعيدةُ
لقد سمعتُ أغنيتَكِ العظيمةَ،
وحلمتُ بنهركِ العظيمِ.
لم أكُن يومًا فاتنةً ولا مُجلجلةَ الحضورِ،
ولا بعيونٍ أثيريّةٍ،
بل تواريتُ في الظّلالِ،
وتركتُ روحي للبديهةِ،
وشَعري على سجيّتِهِ، مسترسِلاً مثل نبعةِ ماءٍ،
لهذا، حظيتُ على فرصتي في الاشتعالِ،
تفجّرتُ،
وصارَ لي نجمٌ في السماءِ من بذورٍ تبعثرتْ منّي،
وصارتْ دليلي.

رآني حبيبي،
وفيَّ استدلَّ إلى قلبِهِ، لم يكُن قد رآهُ قبلَ ذلك.
وكان حبيبي سيّدَ الرجالِ حين قاتلَ لأجلي خفافيشَ العائلة،
وكان سيّدَ الرجالِ حين لفّني بالحريرِ ليلةَ عُرسِنا،
وسيّدَ الرجالِ حين جعلَ ساعدَيهِ سريراً لأجلي،
وسيّدَ الرجالِ حين مات.

اقبليني أيّتُها الأرضُ البعيدةُ،
يمكنُني أن أتشكّلَ مثلما تُحبّينَ:
عودَ ريحانةٍ،
غصنَ رُمّانةٍ،
أغنيةً للبعيدين،

Hala al-Shrouf

Take Me, O Distant Land

Take me, O distant land,
I have heard your exquisite song,
dreamed of your great river.
I was never charming, never flawless,
I didn't have ethereal eyes.
I hid in shadows.
I left my soul to common sense,
I left my hair as it is, waving like waters from a spring.
I got my chance to burn.
I erupted—
the pollen of me dusting into night sky.
Stars were my guides.

My lover saw me.
He found the way to his heart. He hadn't visited it before.
He was the best of men. He fought a family of bats for me,
draped me in silks on our wedding night,
held his forearms out—a bed.
The best of men died when he died.

Accept me, distant land,
I can shape myself as you please—
a basil sprig,
a pomegranate branch,
a song for the far away,

ناراً على رأسِ تلٍّ تدلُّ الغريبَ إليكِ،
أو صخرةً يأخذُها صوتُها الداخليُّ إلى رقّةٍ داخليّة.

غنِّ لي أيّتُها الأرضُ البعيدةُ،
عرفتُ لحنَكِ العظيمَ،
ونسرَكِ العالي فوقَ هضابٍ مَهيبة.
لم أكن يوماً أميرةً ولا سليلَةَ ملوكٍ،
إنّما ابنةَ مُقاتلٍ تركَ لي أن أكونَ ما أشاءُ،
وها أنا قد اخترتُ أن أبدأ المسيرَ إليكِ منذ اليوم،
وحيدةً وعارفة (شاهدة).

الضفة الغربية، ٢٠٢٣

a fire on a hilltop, guiding the stranger to you,
or a stone whose inner voice curls around its tenderness.

Sing to me, distant land,
I recognize your magnificent melody,
an eagle perched high up in the mountains.
I was never a princess, not of royal descent,
but the daughter of the warrior who left me
free to be as I choose.
And here I am, choosing to begin my journey to you today,
alone, knowing, watched.

West Bank, 2023

نهر يشبه الحدس

ضبابٌ كثيفٌ على غيرِ موعدِهِ،
وسربٌ من الطيرِ حطَّ ونام على كتفِ اللّيل،
وبئرٌ من الحظّ، أعرف أسرارَ عتمتِها،
وأُسقِطُ فيها كلامًا عن الحُبّ:
سأحتاجُهُ.

وحين أحدّقُ أكثر، أرى ما يشبهُ حقلاً بعيداً،
إلّا أنّ الضبابَ حجابٌ،
ومن حيث أجلسُ، لا شيءَ يُقشَعُ،
لكنّ حدسي مضيءٌ كمرآة نهرٍ:
أسقِطُ فيه حصىً للتذكُّر:
سأحتاجُهُ.

الضفة الغربية، ٢٠٢٣

A River like Intuition

Thick fog, untimely. A flock alights on the shoulder of night, sleeps.
There's a well of luck. I know its opacity.
I drop love words into its mouth:
I will need them.

Closer—I see what looks like a distant field.
The fog is a veil—
it will not lift from where I'm sitting.
Though my intuition is mirror-bright as a river—
I drop pebbles in, to remember.
I will need them.

West Bank, 2023

سنلتقي، لا تتعجّل أيّ شيء

بعد عشرين ألفَ عامٍ من اليوم، عندما يهدأ هذا العالم،
ومعهُ بؤسُهُ،
بعد أن تخبو نيرانُهُ، ويتعافى من أهوالِهِ التي تبدو الآن وكأنّها لن تنتهي،
بعد أن تعودَ الأرضُ إلى ما كانتْ عليه قبلَ عشرين ألفَ عامٍ من الآن:
خضراءَ بماءٍ أزرقَ وغيومٍ بيضاءَ على الدوامِ،
سنلتقي.

سنأتي كما جئنا أوّلَ مرّةٍ:
بِلا دروعٍ ولا أسلحة،
ولكن بعيونٍ مفتوحةٍ على الروحِ،
عيونٍ سؤالُها مفتاحٌ،
وجوابُها مُستراحٌ،
وكلامُها رحلةٌ في الأثيرِ إلى ما وراءَ الكلامِ،
ولُغاتُها موجاتُ ضوءٍ محمولةٌ في المسافةِ بيني وبينكَ.

سنحتاجُ هذا الوقتَ، وأكثرَ ربّما،
نحتاجُ أن تهدأ البراكينُ،
وتشتعلَ المصابيحُ في سماءٍ أولى وثانيةٍ وثالثة،
وتعودَ الأشجارُ إلى صورتِها الأولى/غاباتٍ لا تنقطع،
والشعاعُ إلى ضوئِهِ الأوّلِ/الضوءِ الذي من ذهبٍ وفضّةٍ/أنا وأنت:
تراني فتسقطُ في يديَّ،
أراكَ فأسقطُ في يديكَ.

الضفة الغربية، ٢٠٢٣

We will meet, don't be in such a rush

In twenty thousand years, when the dust settles on this earth
and the despair, and
its fires burn out, and it recovers from horrors that today seem endless,
and the planet returns to what it was twenty millennia ago—
green with blue water, and white clouds always—
then we will meet.

We will arrive as we did the first time:
without shields, without weapons,
eyes open to the soul,
whose question is a key,
whose answer is a haven,
whose language travels—like waves of light on ether—the distance between us,
beyond speech.

We're going to need that time. Perhaps more.
For the volcanoes to cool,
and lamps to light the first, second, and third skies,
for the trees to reform into forests extending in all directions,
for light rays to return to their source—gold's and silver's light—and you and I:
You will see me and fall into my arms.
I will see you and fall into your arms.

West Bank, 2023

أرى رام الله اثنتين

مطرٌ خفيفٌ في شارع رُكَب، وزينةٌ لمن ينتبه.
رام الله بلادٌ،
ورام الله قديمة، كأنّني عشتُها ألفَ عام،
ورام الله هواءٌ،
وداليةٌ تعربشُ أوراقها فوق قلبي،
وتترك لي سجيّتي مثل تفّاحةٍ فوق رفّ الأواني:
مُهملةً وحُرّة.

ورام الله تحبُّ الذين يحبّون الله كأنّهم يرونَهُ،
وأنا أراه.
ورام الله قريبة،
مثل صوتكَ في مخيّلتي،
مثل أعيادِنا تحت تِينَتِها،
تنزّلُ من سماواتها ملائكةٌ وأعيادٌ لمن ينتبه.
ورام الله قريبة،
مثل وجهي فوق واجهة الزجاج وسط شارع رُكَب:
من هناك أراكَ،
وأرى رام الله اثنتَين:
واحدةً رمّمتني، وواحدةً رفعتني.
ومن هناك، من وراء واجهة الزجاج،
أرى رام الله اثنتَين
تتقابلان فيّ،
وتنظران معًا إليَّ: تلك الفتاة نعرفُها
ونعرفُ أنّنا لم يَرَنا معًا أحدٌ سواها مثلما تفعل الآن.
رام الله ورام الله
تتعانقان،
واحدةٌ تروحُ وراء الكلام السريع،

Two Ramallahs

Light rain on Rukab Street, an embellishment
for those who notice.
Ramallah is a country.
Ramallah is ancient, as if I've lived here millennia.
Ramallah is air.
Grapevines climbing leaves up over my heart,
leaving me my nature. Like an apple on the kitchen's utensil shelf—
Neglected. Free.

Ramallah loves those who love God as if they see Him.
I see Him.
Ramallah is close by.
Like your voice in my imagination.
Like *Eid* under its fig tree.
Angels descend from Ramallah's sky, for those who notice.
Ramallah is nearby.
Like my face pressed up to the shopwindow on Rukab Street.
From there, I see you.
I see Ramallah redoubled:
The city that healed me, the city that elevated me.
In the window, I see two cities
that meet within me,
that look into me: *This girl we see*
alone sees us together.
Ramallah and Ramallah
embrace one another.
One chases after fast talk,

وواحدةٌ تجيء مع الأغاني.
ورام الله جبالٌ،
وعاليةٌ،
وتترك لي أن أراها من شرفة البيت:
مترامية،
فوضويّة،
ومثل كلام الله، بلا خطأ واحدٍ.
مطرٌ خفيفٌ في رام الله، ودفءٌ يسير على قدمَيه لمن ينتبه.

رام الله، ٢٠٢٣

one arrives with songs.
Ramallah is a mountain range,
lofty, visible from the patio—sprawling, chaotic,
like the words of God—flawless.
Gentle rain over Ramallah, warmth underfoot for those who notice it.

Ramallah, 2023

مصعب أبو توهة

لو كنت أعرف

أتسلل إلى حديقة بيتنا
أسترق النظر إلى فنجان قهوتي عبر النافذة.
لا تزال آثار فمي
على الفنجان الأبيض.
لا تزال الساعة تدور بعقاربها
لا تعرف أنها ستداوم على مشاهدة
وجوه غير وجوهنا.
لن يعرف شعورها سوى الجدار.
قلمي لا يزال على مقعد الكتابة،
والصفحات البيضاء تكاد تسقط،
يمسكها الصمت الثقيل كلما هبت ريح
صفراء من جهة الحقول.
لو كنت أعرف، لكتبت على الورقة الأولى:
بيت، بئر، بذور السرو والصنوبر
علّ الريح تُسقط البئر على البيت
فتُسقى البذور ويصير بيتنا
حديقةً أو غابةً
أشاهدها من بعيد
من مخيم اللاجئين.

غزة، ٢٠٢١

Mosab Abu Toha

If I Had Known

I sneak out into our garden,
peek back through the window at my coffee cup,
at the traces of my mouth
on the lip of this white cup.
The clock's hands are still whirling
not knowing—it will watch
faces other than ours.
Only the wall knows how it feels.
My pen is still on my writing desk,
the white sheets are about to fall
into a heavy silence that will hold them
when yellow winds blow in from the fields.
If I had known, I would've written on the first sheet:
House. Well. Cypress. Pine seeds.
May wind coalesce a well above our house, may it cast down its waters
so seeds sprout, and our house sprouts
into a garden, into a forest
that I can see from afar,
that I can see from the refugee camp.

Gaza, 2021

في يوم ميلادي التاسع والعشرين

كيف السماء؟
ككأس شاي سكره خفيف.
وكيف البحر؟
كسريري في العليَّة عندما أنام مفتوح العينين.
وكيف المساء؟
كقهوة ثقيلة.
وكيف الصباح؟
كصوت فيروز عندما تستيقظ من نومها.
وكيف الغيوم؟
كورق الميرمية في كأس الشاي.
وكيف رائحة الهواء؟
كقطف عنب لامس الأرض عندما دخلت قطة بستان الجيران.
وكيف الورق الذي تكتب عليه؟
كسقف بيتنا عندما أتذكرك.
وكيف أنت؟
كما كنت قبل أن أولد.

كتب المؤرخ يوماً:
اليوم هو السابع عشر من نوفمبر.
نسيت السنة.
لا يهم.
لن يقدّم ذلك أو يؤخّر.
أمطرت الغيوم قطرات وجعها في البحر،
والتقطت السماء صورة للأرض بعد البرق،
علقتها على جدران الأنهار البعيدة،
لا يصلها صوت الحجارة وهي تثرثر على الجدران
ولا ضوء شاشات عرض المباريات في الشارع.

My Twenty-Ninth Birthday

How is the sky?
Like a cup of tea, lightly sugared.
And how is the sea?
Like my attic bed when I fall
asleep, eyes still open.
And how is the evening?
Like a strong coffee.
And the morning?
Like Fairuz's voice when she first wakes.
How are the clouds?
Like sage leaves in a glass of tea.
How does the air smell?
Like a bunch of grapes just brushing the ground
when the cat sneaks through the neighbors' orchard.
What about the pages you write on?
Like our roof when you come to mind.
And how are you?
As I was when I was born.

The historian once wrote:
today is November 17.
I almost forgot the year.
It does not matter.
It does not matter.
Clouds pour anguish in droplets out
onto the sea,
and the sky flashes a photograph of the earth,

في هذا اليوم،
خرج ضوءٌ حاجبه كثيف.
تكسَّر بيض الطيور عندما سقطت من الحاجب شعرة.
غرست أوراقُ الخريف رأسها في الأرض.

في هذا اليوم تجمَّعت الحروف على الشاطئ
وبلّل موجُ البحر دقات الساعة المعلّقة في جيب القمر.

في هذا اليوم وزّع بائع الحلوى ما لم يبعه آخر النهار
على الأطفال الجالسين على عتبات منازلهم.

انتهى.
كم بلغت من العمر الآن؟
تسعة وعشرين.
ماذا أنجزت خلالها؟
لا زلت أحاول عد أصابع الشمس
عندما تدخل بيتنا في المخيم،
ولون وجه القمر عندما يخسر
لعبة النرد في البحر،
وملامح وجه ساعتنا
عندما تفرغ البطاريات وتتوقف.

غزة، ٢٠٢١

pins the picture to the walls of far-flung rivers
that neither the chattering stones
nor the light of TV screens from the street can reach.

On this day,
a light with thick eyebrows arched,
and when a hair falls, birds' eggs break.
And autumn leaves bury their heads in the earth.

On this day, letters gather on the shore,
the waves wet the ticking of a timepiece
hanging from the moon's pocket.

At the end of the day, the vendor distributes the unsold candies
to the children sitting on doorsteps.

The end.

How old are you now?
Twenty-nine.
What have you achieved in these years?
I'm still trying to count the sun's fingers
that enter our house in the camp,
and learn the color of the moon's face
when it loses a dice game at sea,
and figure out our clock's facial features
when the batteries run out and it stops.

Gaza, 2021

ما تبقّى

١

كأن رأسي مغطىً بالإبر السوداء،
وكأن ساقيّ جذعُ شجرةٍ تكسوها أهدابٌ رقيقة.

تحطّ ذبابة على أنفي،
تظنّه مهبط طائرات،
أدرك لوهلة أنه صار خشبة تزلج
لعرقٍ تصبَّب بعد تفكير.

أتذكر جاري ذات يومٍ يفتّت ما تبقّى
من حلمه في صحن حساء
يتجمّد كلما وضع فيه قطعة جديدة،
ويغلي عندما يضع شيئاً منه في فمه الصغير.

٢

كان حلمه أن يصبح طياراً.
يحلم أن يطير بالركاب في طائرة
وهو لا يستطيع أن يسافر خارج عتمته،
ولو مشياً.

حاول مرة السفر.
صنع طائرة ورقية.
رسم على الورق خريطة العالم.

أطلق عنان الطائرة على شاطئ البحر.
شعر أنه فوق الهواء،

What Remains

1

It was as if my head were covered in black needles
and my legs were tree trunks with delicate cilia.

A fly landed on my nose
thinking it was an airstrip.
Hang on, it's a skateboard,
sweat pouring out as afterthought.

I recall my neighbor crumbled the leftovers of his dreams
into a bowl of soup.
With each crumb, it froze,
and with each spoonful into his small mouth, it boiled.

2

My friend dreamed of being a pilot, flying passengers in a plane,
but he couldn't travel past his darkness, not even on foot.

He tried traveling once—
Made a paper plane,
drew on it the world map.

Threw it over the seashore,
fancied he was above air,
above stars,
nearing the moon.

فوق النجوم،
أنه اقترب من القمر.

رصاصتان من قارب على الجانب الآخر
رصاصة ثقبت قلب الطائرة،
وأخرى حلم الطيار الهشّ.
كم كان يتمنى أن يرى بطائرته القطب الشمالي.
سقطت طائرته وانهمرت ثلوج حارّة على وجهه.
سقط مُغمىً عليه.

أطفال على الشاطئ عبثاً يصلحون الطائرة
يحاولون رقع العالم.
كان الخرق كبيراً.
ذابت دولٌ كثيرة.
بحثوا عن صندوق الطائرة الأسود.
لم يجدوه.

دفن الأطفال الطائرة الورقية قرب عمودٍ
تبقّى من المطار المدمر.

تكوّمت حمامات المدينة ليلاً
تبكي على قبر الطائرة.

غزة، ٢٠٢١

Then two bullets from a boat off the other bank.
One bullet pierced the plane's heart.
The other, the pilot's delicate dream—
he wished he could see the North Pole from his plane—
it crashed, hot snow falling on his face.
He fell unconscious.

On the beach, the children tried in vain to fix it.
Tried to patch up the world,
but the rupture is vast
and countries are dissolving.
They searched for the black box
but didn't find it.

So the children buried the plane near a pole—
all that remains of the airport, razed to the ground.

At night, the city doves gather
to mourn at the airplane's grave.

Gaza, 2021

ياسر الوقّاد

انتشالُ غدي من ركام المتاهة

يتنفَّسُ القتلى الحصى والحنطة
الأشجارُ أعمدةٌ من الكبريتِ، وجهُكَ
أيها المجنونُ شاحنةٌ تحمل طحينَها
للنازحينَ، وفي الطريقِ سطا عليها أغنياءُ
ومُعدمونَ، وبيعَ كلُّ طحينِها في الشارعِ
العام، الغيومُ رسائلُ، الموتى بيادرُ،
أَضلعي جدرانُ مكتبةٍ أمامَ تَوَحُّشِ
الجرَّافةِ، الجيشُ الحقيرُ يشدُّ شريانَ المدينةِ،
كان ممتلئاً بأطفالِ السماءِ،
وكان أكبرَ من مجرَّتنا
وأَسمى.

ماذا تفيدُ خيامُكم يا أيها الثَّمِلونَ؟
كلُّ تذاكرِ التيهِ التي تُهدونَها مزَّعْتُها،
والآنَ أبني في رمالِ الوعي مئذنتي الأخيرةَ،
واقفًا بفَمِ المسافةِ مثلَ بسملةِ النخيلِ،
ولا أُبالي بالخيامِ وبالرَّحيلِ؛
فإنَّ أمسي يطمئنُّ بقبرِهِ،
وغدي أُشَيّدهُ بآنيةِ العَناءِ وسُكَّرِ المعنى،
وأهنأُ، فالغدُ الأُمميُّ عارٌ عابسُ الوجهينِ
أعمى.

غزة، ٢٠٢٤

Yasir al-Waqqad

Pulling my tomorrow out of the maze's rubble

The murdered inhale wheat and gravel,
the trees are matchstick plumes, your face,
oh lunatic, a truck carrying flour for
refugees, on its way stolen by the rich
and wretched, who sell on the street, flour.
Clouds are messages, the dead a threshing floor,
my rib cage a library before the brutal bull-
dozer, the bastard army constricting the city's arteries,
once swarming with the children of heaven.
Gaza was larger than our galaxy,
and nobler.

What good are your tents, you drunkards?
I've torn them all up, the tickets you've given me,
and now I build in these sands of consciousness my last minaret
and stand in the mouth of space like a date palm: *in the name of God,*
the most compassionate, the most merciful,
I don't care for tents or for flight.
Yesterday rests in its grave,
and I meet my tomorrow with pain's knife and fork,
and the sugar of meaning.
I rejoice. The world's tomorrow is a shame—
frowning, blind, two-faced.

Gaza, 2024

قصة حذائي العتيق

حذائي العتيقُ الذي خلّفته
بين أمتعةِ البيتِ
عندما باغَتَتْنا القذائفُ
قابَلْتُهُ
عند بيّاعِ أحذيةٍ
في مخيمنا الرَّفَحي الغريقْ
بأدخنةٍ للهوانِ،
وأَكْثِبَةٍ للأسى: مَن أتى بكَ؟
هل جئتَ تتبعُني، وضللتَ الطريقْ؟
أرى دمعتينِ بقلبي تقطَّرتا،
غيمتينِ بذهني ترقّطتا،
وتَصاعُدَ نيرانِ أسئلةٍ من سراجي الذبيحِ البريقْ
سأسألُ عن سعره،
فيغمغمُ بائعُه: «بثمانينَ شيكلَ،
هل تشتريهِ؟»

أنا؟
أشتريه؟
ولكنَّه، أيها التافهونَ، حذائي،
ويعرفني منذُ أزمنةٍ.
منه أدنو،
وأمسحُ عنه الغبارَ،
وأكشفُ جلدَ الحذاءِ العريقْ
فتبدو به السُّبُلُ الجبليَّةُ طرَّزْتُـها بخطايَ الفتيَّةِ،
تبدو به الدَّرجاتُ التي تتصاعدُ

The Story of My Old Shoes

I left my old shoes
with all our belongings
when the shelling
caught us off guard,

but came upon them again
at the shoe seller's
in the Rafah refugee camp,
in the smoke of humiliation,
in the sands of sorrow: *Who brought you here?*

Did you follow after me and lose your way?
Two tears roll down my heart,
two speckled clouds in my head.
Burning questions rise from my
slain oil lamp and scintillate,
I will ask the price.
The salesman mumbles, "Eighty shekels,
will you get them?"

"Me? Buy them?
They are my shoes, you petty people."
The pair's known me forever.

Now I approach them,
I wipe dust from their old leather,
from the mountain passes I embroidered

للقاعةِ الشاعريةِ،
تبدو به بُقعة الحبرِ.
كَم مِن مدادٍ على أبجديَّةِ أمسي
أريق!

أُكَلمُه،
قبضةُ البائعِ النذْلِ تدفعني،
والمشاةُ يَدُعُّونَني،
وأنا قصةٌ برتقاليَّةٌ تَتَرَنَّحُ يقظى وسكرانةً
بين عارِ الخيامِ
وعُهر الحريقْ.

غزة، ٢٠٢٤

with my footsteps, and up the stairs,
and into the poetry auditorium.
I touch them. There is an ink stain,
yesterday's alphabet.

I spoke with them like this,
until the peddler shoved me off.
I am a story in amber, staggering,
conscious, drunk,
here, between the shame of the camp
and hellfire.

Gaza, 2024

عملية في جسد الحلم

صيارفةُ الطين
يلتهمون الأزقَّةَ والشارعَ العامَّ،
والنملُ ينسلُّ من قبضة الوحْل مُلتجئاً
مثل عائلة الأبجديةْ
إلى جسدي المتهالكِ؛
حتى يؤسسَ في طعنةٍ فيه زنبقةً
مَعْبَدِيَّـةْ.

أقاومُ ميليشيا الريحِ،
أَكتظُّ بالأَثْلِ والسرْوِ، حتى
بتمتمة الشيحِ،
أنحاز لله في حلكةِ الجاهليَّةِ،
أدرأُ عني صيارفةَ الطينِ،
ألعنُ كلَّ (مؤسسةٍ) ترجمتني إلى غيّها،
وأقاومُ حتى أزيلَ من الحلْم ما أدْخَلتْهُ المدينةُ
في لحمه من جنودٍ وأكياس رملٍ وأوبئة زَرَديّة.

أقاومُ مستنقعاتِك
يا أيها العالَمُ النذلُ
مُنتشلاً من دناستها سَمَكي البرتقاليَّ،
والعشبة البرية، والليلكَ المشتهى
بيديَّهْ.

هنا لي انتسابي،
فمن شاءني صاحباً وأخاً
فليعانقْ ببريَّةِ الوعي أولَ سنبلةٍ
تتفقّه من حكمة الطين، وليستمدَّ المعارفَ

Surgery on the Dream Body

The clay capitalist
feeds on the alleys, the main street—
ants swarm from his grip,
taking refuge like the alphabet
in my decrepit body.
From a stab wound grows a temple lily.

I resist the militia hidden in the wind. I over-
flow with tamarisk, cypress,
mutterings of worm-
wood. I side with God
in the dark of ignorance.
I fend off the capitalist.
I curse every superstructure
translating me into its ill intent.
I resist. I dream,
until I can extract from the city what has been implanted in its flesh—
sandbags, soldiers, insatiable plagues.

I resist your quagmire, loathsome world.
I use my hands. I pluck from this filth
my little goldfish,
wild herbs,
coveted lilacs.

This is where I belong.
Whoever wants me as their friend, as their brother,

من أي جَدَّةٍ كِينا تظللُ أسْفَلتَنا
وخسارتنا (الـمقْعَدِيَّةْ) القديمة.

على الياسـمين احتسابي
شهيدَ أغانيه، أما المساميرُ في رئتي
فلْتكنْ أَغْصُناً للمنارةِ تُبدي قناديلَها البُرْعُمِيَّةَ
أسئلةً أبَدِيَّةْ.

غزة، ٢٠٢٤

should seek out the spike of wheat in their wilderness of mind.
Should learn the mud's philosophy, should draw wisdom
from our ancestor the eucalyptus,
from the paved road.

Now the jasmine must acknowledge me.
On the jasmine, I rest my case.
I am a martyr to its scent. With its nails in my lungs,
let it build a lighthouse. Its lamp will brighten over
these interminable reflections.

Gaza, 2024

غسان زقطان

التماثيل والأبواب

لا بد أن يكون لهذه المدينة باب
الطوّافون في أزقتها وعارفو سراديبها لم يهتدوا بعد لأبوابها.

كلّما حفروا في الأرض وجدوا تمثالاً ميتاً
كلّما دقّوا على جدار يخرج تمثال أعمى.

الخلق الذين وجدوا أنفسهم داخل أسوارها المغلقة وبيوتها الضيقة يواصلون السعي في الأسواق
ويدقون على أعمدة الساحات وتماثيل قادة ممجّدين
لم يذهبوا إلى الحرب
لا أحد يتذكر القادة ولا معاركهم
لا أحد يعرف مآثرهم.

ليس ثمّة ما يمكن شراؤه هنا
ليس ثمّة من يبيع ومن يشتري

ولكنّه، السوق، مليء بالنداءات وأصوات الدلّالين
أصوات لا غير.

الرجل الخائف الذي توقف عن النوم يروي كوابيسه على المارة
بينما التماثيل تواصل تسلّق الأدراج.

التماثيل وصلت قبل الناس
كانت هنا قبل المدينة وقبل الأسوار، يقول الرجل الخائف.

Ghassan Zaqtan

Statues and Gates

This city must have a gate,
but those who wander its alleys and crypts have not found it yet.

Whenever they dig deep into the ground, they find a dead statue.
Whenever they bang on a wall, a blind statue walks out.

People who find themselves lost within its doorless walls
are always strolling through the marketplace,
knocking on the square's columns, knocking on the statues of glorified leaders
who never went to war.
No one can remember them or their battles.
No one can remember their feats.

There's nothing to buy here.
There are no buyers and no sellers.

But it's a market, full of calls, brokers' voices,
nothing else. Just voices.

The frightened man who's stopped sleeping recounts his nightmares to passersby.
While statues keep on climbing upstairs.

The statues arrived here before the people.
They came even before the city, before the walls, says the frightened man.

في الليل نسمع جلبة بنّائين لا نراهم، تقول امرأة من العامّة في السوق،
وفي الصباح نجد تماثيل جديدة، تكمل المرأة.

التماثيل تصعد الأدراج وتقف على عتبات المنازل
وتحدّق بعيونها الميتة من النوافذ.

علينا أن نتذكّر أولاً، تقول المرأة في السوق
علينا أن نتذكّر، تكرر المرأة.

الضفة الغربية، ٢٠٢٤

In the market a laywoman says, *At night we hear the clamor of stonemasons, but we don't see them.*
In the morning, we find the new statues, the woman continues.

Statues climb up doorsteps. They stand on the houses' verandas.
They stare into the windows at their dead eyes.

First, we must remember, says that woman in the market.
We must remember, she repeats.

West Bank, 2024

أيها النصر

أيها النصر
أيها الصنم الذي ينزف كل ليلة على عتبات بيوتنا
ويترك دمه في أحلامنا.

أيها الشبح الذي يسحب ظلّه في الوديان مثل عربة أحجار سوداء
وهو ينادينا بأسماء أمهاتنا.

يا جدول الدم
النازل من بيوت أجدادنا المحفورة في الجبال العالية
نحو حصائرنا المفرودة في منافينا
القادم من تلال الزمن العميقة وشقوق الحكاية الأولى
ليصب في أيامنا المعقودة على المشقة وموت الإخوة.

أيها الضبع
التي تنادي أولادنا كلما غفوا وتقودهم مسرنمين إلى مسالك الجبال الشائكة
خفخفتك التي تأخذنا
وضحكتك التي تنبت فيها الحجارة والأيام القاسية
خطوتك التي تسبقنا
وظلك ما نجده على المصاطب.

أيها النصر
الرجل العالق في المنعطف
والشجرة في السفح
والطائر في الزوبعة
الضوء في المقبرة
والأثر على الرمل
والأمل الذي يربي الموت في حديقته.

O Victory

O victory,
fetish bleeding on our doorsteps every night,
leaving your blood in our dreams,

ghost hauling your shadow into the valley—
wheelbarrow full of black stones
calling to us with our mothers' names.

O river of blood, flowing
from our grandparents' abandoned homes in the high mountains
toward mats spread over
the hills of deep time, over the cracks in the first tale,
over our days of toil and the death of brothers.

O hyena,
yapping at our children as they doze off, leading them
onto the thorny mountain pass.
Your yowling pursues us,
your tracks precede us,
we find your shadows on the slopes.

O victory,
the man at the forking road,
the tree at the foothill,
the bird in the whirlwind,
the light in the graveyard,
the trace in the sand,
and hope in its garden fostering death.

أيها النصر
نحن حبّ الرحى
في حديث الغبار.

حملنا على أكتافنا نهرنا العزيز وبحيراتنا الغالية
كمن يحمل معجزات الخلق عن كاهل الرسل
في كل ماء معجزة وعلى كل أرض مقتلة.

أيها النصر
نحن الذين بعَثَتنا اليكَ الولاياتُ
بالذهبِ وكُتبِ الموتى،
مَكَثْنا في الدروبِ والحاناتِ
أثْقَلْنا الأدلّاءَ بالعطايا
وعلَّقْنا الحريرَ على الخرائبِ
وبالتذّكرِ أغلَقْنا عيون الموتى
وليس لنا ملكٌ
ولا قضاة.

الضفة الغربية، ٢٠٢٤

O victory,
we are the millstones' grain,
the speech of dust.
We carry on our shoulders our dear river, our precious lakes,
we are conveying earth's miracles for the prophets.
In all water, there's marvel. In every land, there's carnage.

O victory,
we have been sent to you by the nations
with gold and the books of the dead.
We stay for a while on the road, and in the pubs,
we burden our guides with gifts,
we hang silk over the ruins,
with memories, we close the dead's eyes.
We have no kings and no judges.

West Bank, 2024

تسعة أولاد وبنت

بعينينِ واسعتينِ وشَعرٍ قَصيرٍ

في الذاكرةِ، ولدٌ بعينينِ واسعتينِ وشَعرٍ قَصير
هوَ الولدُ الذي ماتت شقيقتهُ في الصفِّ الرابعِ
يصلُ قبل الجميعِ وينتظرُ بصبرٍ
الولدُ الذي يُحضِرُ الكرةَ عندما تطيرُ بعيداً
الذي يضعُ حجراً على ملابسِ اللاعبينَ وكُتبهم لئلّا يُطيّرَها الهواءُ القادمُ من النهر
الهواءُ البطيءُ بسبب رائحةِ الجوّافةِ
السعيدُ لأنّ أشجارَ الليمون القريبةَ من النهرِ أطلقت أزهارَها
الخفيفُ لأنه مرَّ على أحواضِ النعناعِ.

الولدُ الذي يحرسُ الحجرَ
ويحرسُ الحقائبَ
ويُحضِرُ الماءَ
ويُسجّلُ الأهدافَ على باطنِ كفِّهِ بقلم «كوبيا».

بكتفينِ نحيلتينِ وأصابعَ طويلة

ثمّةَ ولدٌ بكتفينِ نحيلتينِ وأصابعَ طويلةٍ
هوَ الولدُ الأوّلُ
يضحكُ على الحكاياتِ المُعادةِ
والمغامراتِ البائسةِ
وبطولاتٍ طائشةٍ بلا شهودٍ
ويحفظُ تفاصيلَ صغيرةً لترميم ثغراتِ رواةٍ أخذتهم الحماسةُ
يصغي بقلبه المهتمّ ودهشةِ عينيهِ لأغنيةٍ عبثَ بلازمتها الكورسُ

Nine Sons and One Daughter

With two large eyes and short hair

In the memory, a boy with large eyes and short hair,
whose sister died in fourth grade,
arrives before everyone else, waits patiently,
fetches the ball when it flies away,
places a rock on each player's clothes and books
so wind rising from the river won't blow them away.
The air is slowed by the smell of guava,
cheered by the lemon trees at the river, unleashing blossoms,
and lightened by the beds of mint.

The boy who guards the rock,
guards the bags,
brings water,
scores goals on his palm with an indelible pencil.

With scrawny shoulders and long fingers

There is a boy with scrawny shoulders and long fingers,
the eldest son in his family.
He laughs at the same stories, told over again—
hapless adventures,
reckless heroisms, unwitnessed,
he memorizes minute details to patch up gaps for overzealous narrators.
He listens with an attentive heart and wide eyes to a song,
whose chorus messed up its refrain.

ويضحكُ
ويضحكُ
ويواصلُ الضَحك حتّى يستلقيَ على ظهره
ويتودّدُ لكلّ شيء.

بغمازتينِ وحاجبينِ كثيفينِ

ثمّةَ ولدٌ يشبهُ شقيقتهُ التي قتلتها الملاريا
بغمّازتينِ وحاجبينِ كثيفينِ
هوَ الولدُ الأوّلُ والثاني
يحتفظُ بعلبة كبريتٍ ولا يدخّنُ
يتطوّعُ ليشتريَ السجائرَ الممنوعةَ من الحانوتِ الأبعدِ
أينَ يعيشُ تاجرٌ بدينٌ
وابنتهُ الغيورةُ الماكرةُ
وحيثُ تواصلُ زوجتُه الصامتةُ قليَ الفلافلِ للتلاميذِ والمارّةِ وعُمّال الزراعةِ
بينما تتنفَّسُ على المصطبةِ
ثلاثةُ كلابٍ كسولة.

بقميصٍ مشجَّرٍ وحذاءٍ واسع

ثمّةَ ولدٌ يَظهرُ من دغلِ أشجارِ «الطَّرفة»
بقميصٍ مشجَّرٍ وحذاءٍ واسع
هوَ الأولادُ الثلاثةُ
يطرفُ بعينيهِ ويقوّسُ ساقيهِ
وهوَ يقلّدُ الجنادبَ في حقولِ الذرةِ
والضفادعَ على قنواتِ الريّ
يتمدّدُ قربَ أكمةِ القصبِ على ضفّةِ النهرِ
ينظرُ إلى السابحينَ العُراةِ
ويَحرسُ أسمالَهم
ويُطلقُ على الأشياءِ ألقاباً ماجنةً.

And he laughs
and laughs,
and keeps laughing
until he's fawning over everything,
until he's lying on his back.

With two dimples and bushy eyebrows

There is a boy who looks like his sister—she died of malaria—
with two dimples and bushy eyebrows.
He is the first and second son in one.
He keeps a box of matches. He doesn't smoke.
Volunteers to buy forbidden cigarettes from the farthest store
where the fat merchant lives,
and his jealous, cunning daughter.
Where his silent wife keeps frying falafel for students, pedestrians, for farmworkers.
Breathing on the veranda,
three lazy dogs.

With a floral shirt and baggy shoes

A boy emerges from the tamarisk trees
in a floral shirt and baggy shoes.
He is all three boys combined.
He blinks his eyes and bends his legs
imitating the grasshoppers in cornfields,
the frogs in aqueducts.
He lies back on the riverbank by the reeds,
watching swimmers skinny-dip
guarding their shabby clothes.
He gives each thing its dirty nickname.

بصوتٍ مبحوحٍ وضحكةٍ قديمةٍ

ثمّةَ ولدٌ بصوتٍ مبحوحٍ وضحكةٍ قديمة
هوَ الأولادُ الأربعةُ
الذي بكى في جنازةِ شقيقتهِ مثلَ البناتِ
يحملُ الرسائلَ المطويّةَ على الولَه لبنات المدرسةِ المجاورةِ
أينَ يكمنُ حارسٌ مسنٌّ
وآذنٌ غضوبٌ
ومعلّماتٌ ضَجراتٌ.
ويقطفُ زهوراً لبناتِ الجيرانِ
حيثُ يطوفُ آباءٌ حذرون
وأمّهاتٌ يُبصِرن في العتمة.

بوجهٍ شاحبٍ وعينينِ لامعتينِ

ثمّةَ ولدٌ ينهضُ قبلَ الجميعِ
بوجهٍ شاحبٍ وعينينِ لامعتينِ
هوَ الأولادُ الخمسةُ
يقرأُ درسَ اللغةِ العربيّةِ بمشقة
ويُخطئ في جدولِ الضربِ
ورموزِ العناصرِ
وغزوةِ الخندقِ
ويكتبُ خرابيشَ الدجاجِ
ويقضي أوقاتَ الفُرصِ في زاويةِ القَصاصِ
وهو يرمشُ وحيداً بعينيه البُنيّتين.

With a hoarse voice and an ancient laugh

There is a boy with a hoarse voice and an ancient laugh
who is now four boys combined
and cries like a girl at his sister's funeral.
He carries folded love letters to girls at his sister school.
There is an old guard,
there is a hot-tempered janitor,
there are bored teachers.
He picks flowers for the girls next door,
where cautious fathers roam
and mothers see in the dark.

With a pale face and bright eyes

There is a boy who rises before everyone else
with a pale face and bright eyes.
He is the one who is five kids combined.
He struggles to read his Arabic,
adds mistakes to the times table
and the periodic,
and to the Battle of the Trench.
Writes in chickens' scratchings,
spends his recess in time-out.
Alone in the corner,
blinking his brown eyes.

بأسنانٍ بارزةٍ ولثغةٍ ضاحكة

ثمّةَ ولدٌ يصلُ قبل الجميعِ
بأسنانٍ بارزةٍ ولثغةٍ ضاحكةٍ
الولدُ الذي دفنّا شقيقتهُ الصغيرةَ تحت شجرةِ دِفلى
هوَ الأولادُ الستّةُ
يقفزُ في دروبِ البيّاراتِ
يتفقّدُ ثمارَ الجوّافةِ الناضجةَ
وقطوفَ الموزِ القريبةَ من السياجِ
يطلقُ أسماءً بشريّةً على الأشجارِ
الحلاّقَ وحارسَ مدرسةِ البناتِ وبائعةَ الفلافل وزوجَها البدين . . .
أستاذَ اللغةِ العربيةِ وسائقَ سيّارةِ الإسعافِ وممرّضةَ العيادةِ المرحةَ . . .
شيخَ الجامعِ وشاويشَ المخفرِ والمُخبرَ الذي اشترى نظّارةً جديدةً . . .
صاحبَ المقهى ومُؤجّرَ الدرّاجاتِ وابنةَ الفرّانِ الشقراءَ
يتركُ أسماءَهم على الأشجارِ التي ستُشبهُهم منذ الآنَ
وستتبعُهم في الحاراتِ إلى عَتبات بيوتِهم
وتقفُ خلفَ نوافذِهم وهي تبتسمُ.

ثمّ يبني أفكاراً لسرقاتِ الليلِ
وخدائعَ للنواطيرِ.

برقبةٍ نحيلةٍ وبشرةٍ غامقة

ثمّةَ ولدٌ يبدأُ قبل الجميعِ
برقبةٍ نحيلةٍ وبشرةٍ غامقة
هو الأولادُ السبعةُ
ينعسُ في الحرّ وحصصِ التاريخِ وأيّامِ الصيامِ الطويلةِ
فينحلُ في النوم
وتذبلُ الأوراقُ فوقَ قميصهِ المشجّرِ
وتميلُ رقبتُه الطويلةُ على كتفه
مثلَ طيورِ الماءِ.

With buckteeth and a laughing lisp

A boy arrives before everyone else
with buckteeth and a laughing lisp.
We buried his little sister beneath the oleander.
He is six boys in one
hopping up the orchard paths
inspecting a ripe guava,
bunches of bananas dangling by the fence.
He gives the trees human names—
the barber, the guard at the girls' school, the falafel vendor, her plump husband . . .
the Arabic teacher, the ambulance driver, the jolly clinic nurse . . .
the sheikh of the mosque, the police inspector, and his informant who just bought a new pair of glasses . . .
The café owner, bicycle renter, and the baker's blond daughter.
They bequeath their names to the trees who will resemble them from now on.
They will haunt the alleys up through to their doorsteps.
They stand behind the windows, smiling.

So the boy draws up nighttime plans for robbers.
He has to find ways to trick the guards.

With a slender neck and dark skin

There is a boy who starts the day before everybody else,
with a slender neck and dark complexion.
He is seven children.
He dozes off in the heat, in history class, on long days of fasting.
As he sleeps, he wastes away,
the leaves wither on his floral shirt,
his long neck tilts over his shoulder
like a waterbird.

بساقينِ من قصبٍ ورُكبةٍ مجرّحة

ثمّةَ ولدٌ بساقين من قصبٍ ورُكبةٍ مجرَّحة
الولدُ الذي وضعَ تفّاحةً على قبرِ شقيقتهِ
وشريطاً ملوّناً لتربطَ شعرَها.
هو الأولادُ الثمانيةُ
ذهبَ قبلَ الجميعِ
قفزَ عن الجدارِ
وتركَ ثغرةً في كلّ شيءٍ
منها يدخلُ الحُبُّ والأسى
والحظوظُ الضائعةُ.

الضفة الغربية، ٢٠٢٤

With legs of reed and a bruised knee

There is a boy with legs of reed and a bruised knee.
He places an apple on his sister's grave,
and a colorful ribbon to tie her hair.
He is eight boys.
He goes before everyone else.
He jumps off the wall.
He leaves a hole in everything
through which love and sorrow
and lost fortune seep.

West Bank, 2024

أغنّي لأكثّر انتظاري

أغنّي لأكثّر انتظاري
ليسمعَني الأولادُ العائدون من البساتين بثمارٍ مسروقةٍ
ويهتديَ الدراويشُ الذين علقوا في المدائح
والنِعم المتدفّقة كالأنهارِ في أجسادِهم المتروكةِ للبركة
والنساءُ المنسيّات تحتَ أحمالِ الحطبِ في دروب تتجدّد تحتَ أقدامِهنّ المشقّقة ولا تصل
لتستطيلَ جدائلُ البنات المقتولات في الخرائبِ وتتلوّنَ خدودهنّ التي بيّضتها العتمةُ.

أغنّي لتتعشّى العائلةُ
ويتلفّت الغزالُ
وتصلَ رسالةُ الغائب
ويغطّيَ الأبُ نومَ ابنته التي تضحك في حلُمِها
أغنّي ولا أسمعُ صوتي
لكنّني أبصرُه وهو يطوفُ على التلال والخرائب مثل غيمةِ مناديل.

الضفة الغربية، ٢٠٢٤

I sing so I can wait longer

so children returning from the orchard with stolen fruit might hear
and those dervishes stranded in prayer—
grace pouring a river into their bodies—
their bodies offered as blessing. And forgotten
women balancing bundles of firewood
on their heads
reviving the paths under their cracked feet.
They never arrive.
Their dead daughters' braids grow longer under the rubble. Their cheeks grow
whiter in the dark.

I sing to feed the family dinner,
I sing so the gazelle will turn around,
I sing so the missing person's message will arrive.
A father pulls a cover over his sleeping daughter,
she's laughing in her dream.
I sing. I don't hear my own voice.
I see it. Floating over the hills and ruins like a cloud of handkerchiefs.

West Bank, 2024

فداء زياد

في البال أغنية واحدة

منذ الصباح لم تسكت
لم تتوقّف
كلما مشيت أسمع طنينها كالنحلة في أذني
وكلما تجاهلتها وأنا أجادل البائع سعر مسحوق الغسيل
قفزت كنبض قلبي
كلما تحدثت إلى النساء من شبابيك البيت
عادت كالصدى

وكلما أثنيت على ولد لقوة عضلاته
وابتسمت لبنت تنتظر عيد ميلادها
وركلت الحجر في طريقي
ألقت بنفسها في وجهي
وكلما مضيت أغسل وجهي
لمحتها في المرآة

وكلما انشغلت بتقطيع ورق النص الرديء
جلست أمامي تهزّ قدميها
في البال أغنية
أعرفها.
أسمعها تطن
ليست هنا في قائمة الموسيقى الخاصة بي!
ولم ألمحها كهدية من صديق
لكنها تهاجمني منذ الصباح
تضرب رأسي
أتجاهلها

Fida'a Zayed

A Song Comes to Mind

Since morning, the drone hasn't shut up.
It won't stop.
Wherever I walk I hear its buzzing.
If I forget, arguing with a vendor over the price of detergent,
it only leaps back quick with my heartbeat.
While I chat with women through windows,
it rebounds, echoing.

If I praise a boy for his muscles,
or smile at a girl waiting for her birthday,
or kick a stone down my path,
it will only fly back into my face.
And whenever I wash my face,
I spot it in the mirror.

And when I'm busy tearing up bad writing,
it perches itself before me,
shaking and shaking.
Then a song comes to mind.
I recognize it,
hear its humming,
I know it's not on my playlist,
I know it's not a friend's gift,
it's been harassing me since morning,
it's been driving into my head.

تفور في غلاية القهوة
أنقذت يدي من احتراقها.

ترك لي الأصدقاء أيديهم بلا وداع
وتركت لي إحداهن اليوم وصيتها في رسالة
فانفجرت الأغنية
من عيني!
أغنية منذ الصباح في البال
صارت محض بكاء!

غزة، ٢٠٢٤

But I will ignore it.
I will say it is only the bubbling in a coffeepot.
Look, its song saves my hand from getting burned.

Meanwhile friends leave me their hands, without a goodbye.
Today, one messaged me her will.
And the song bursts in my eyes.
I cannot dislodge it from my head.
And it is still just morning.
Just morning.

Gaza, 2024

Biographical Notes

Amal Abu Qamar has a bachelor's degree in Arabic language and teaching methods. She contributed poetry to *Gaza, terra da poesia* (2022).

Mosab Abu Toha is a Palestinian poet, short story writer, and essayist from Gaza. His first collection of poetry, *Things You May Find Hidden in My Ear,* was a finalist for the National Book Critics Circle Award and won the Palestine Book Award, the American Book Award, and the Derek Walcott Poetry Prize. Mosab is also the founder of the Edward Said Public Library in Gaza. He won an Overseas Press Club Award in 2023 and a Pulitzer Prize for Commentary in 2025 for his Letter from Gaza columns for *The New Yorker.* His writings from Gaza have appeared in *The Nation, The New York Times, The Washington Post, The Atlantic,* and *The New York Review of Books,* among others. His second poetry book, *Forest of Noise,* was published by Knopf in 2024. Photo by Mohammed Mahdy.

Jawad al-Aqqad is a Palestinian poet and writer, a scholar of Arab thought, and the editor in chief of the online newspaper *Al-Yamama al-Jadida.* In 2023, he published a book of criticism, *Reflections on Aesthetic Sufism,* and a collection of poems, *The Stations of Whiteness.* In 2017, he published *On Ishtar's Account,* a collection of poems. In addition to his books, Jawad writes articles and essays for several newspapers and magazines, particularly the Editor's Opinion column in *Al-Yamama al-Jadida.* Jawad is currently documenting his harrowing displacement during the 2023 Gaza War.

Waleed al-Aqqad, born in Gaza in 1992, is a Palestinian poet, playwright, and short story writer. He graduated from the faculty of media at the University of Palestine. Waleed contributed poetry to *The Apple of Poetry,* which was longlisted for the Ibrahim Jabra Award, and fiction to *Assassination of a Memory: A Collection of the Nakba Stories,* published in collaboration with the Society of Culture and Free Thought. His poetry also appeared in the folio of recent poems from Gaza in the 2021 edition of the Harvard literary magazine *Peripheries: Journal of Word, Image, and Sound,* guest-edited by Mosab Abu Toha and Tayseer Abu Odeh. Waleed was awarded second place in the Innovations Competition, fifth place in the Abdul Hamid al-Karmi Short Story Award, and first place in the University of Palestine's Playwriting Competition.

Author's note: Writing, for me, is like breathing—an action of life and survival. Internalized, poetry becomes a private space where I can invent my own freedoms. I can run freely over its lines, across the page. I run far from the whizzing bullets and the blades of bulldozers. In the poem, no one seizes me by the throat. I can rest. I can look out through the window of poetry at the world. I look out at Gaza. I search it. Our elimination . . .

I must use poetry to paint this world with the brushes of utopia *and* dystopia. Use my imagination to nurture hope, to invent words in lieu of those that have gone missing. I must write to immortalize the horror of Palestinian suffering and to resist oblivion.

Born in Nablus in the northern West Bank in 1984, **Tariq al-Arabi** still lives and works in the same city. He has a bachelor's degree in journalism from the An-Najah National University and publishes articles and poems in Palestinian magazines. He has participated in the Mediterranean Poetry Festival, and his poems have been translated into English, French, and Spanish. His poetry collection *4am in the Market* won the Qattan Foundation Young Writer Award for 2012, jointly with *What If We Were Ghosts?* by Samar Abdel Jaber.

Hamid Ashour was born in 1994 in Rafah, Gaza, Palestine. He has a bachelor's degree in social and family development from Al-Quds Open University. His published works include the poetry collections *Wounds Test Themselves* (2018) and *This Product Cannot Be Exchanged or Returned* (2023).

Yahya Ashour is an exiled Gazan touring poet and awarded author, born in 1998 and currently based in America. He is the author of the e-book *A Gaza of Siege & Genocide* (2024). Ashour's publications include a poetry collection and two children's books in Arabic. His work has been featured in several anthologies and journals, including the *Michigan Quarterly Review* and *ArabLit*. His poetry manuscript-in-progress got an honorable mention from the Miami Book Fair's Emerging Writer Fellowship. He has read poetry at several organizations and thirty-five US universities, including Princeton, Stanford, UPenn, and UCLA. His poetry has been translated into several languages, including Spanish, French, Japanese, and Bengali. Ashour studied sociology and psychology and was a creative writing mentor in Gaza.

Nasser Atallah, born in Damascus in 1967, is a Palestinian poet and writer. He has published several collections of poetry, most recently *The Widow of Absence.* Previous collections include *This Is What Concerns Me* (2020), *What the Stranger Said* (2016), and *Does the Rose Suffice?* (2003). He has also published fiction, *The Desert of Life,* and travel writing, *Temporary Freedom.* His autobiography, *A Second Shadow,* is forthcoming. Nasser was named Cultural Personality of the Year (2021) by the Palestinian Ministry of Culture and received the Freedom PEN Award (2019).

Nidal al-Faqaawi is a Palestinian poet, born in 1985 in Khan Yunis, Gaza. Nidal's first published poetry collection, *Noon: Poems in a Cobbler's Cart,* shared first prize in the Young Writer Competition (2015). Nidal's poems have been published in various literary journals and online platforms, including the local magazine *Ishtar* and the regional magazine *28.* Nidal has a second manuscript of poetry that he hopes to publish.

Author's note: During the recent war on Gaza, Israeli forces occupied my private library and poetry retreat on the rooftop of my house. After their departure, they burned my home, destroying all my writings. I have been living in a carpentry workshop for the past five months. There, I continue to write poems and compile my war diaries whenever I can.

Anes Ganema, born in Gaza, Palestine, is a poet, web programmer, and entrepreneur. He is winner of the Young Writer Poetry Prize (2017) and has been published in numerous cultural journals and newspapers, including *Mizna, ArabPop, Al-Araby al-Jadeed, Fus'ha, 28* (a Palestinian magazine), *Al-Akhbar* (Lebanon), and *Al-Antologia,* and he is the author of *The Funeral of a Magician* (2017).

Haider al-Ghazali is a young poet and cultural editor at *Al-Yamama al-Jadida* newspaper, completing his bachelor's in English literature. He is a member of the editorial team of the Yar'aat literary group and of creative writing clubs in Gaza. He was awarded third place in the Jabra Ibrahim Jabra Poetry Competition (2021).

Born in 1967 in Al-Shati Camp, Gaza, **Ala'a al-Ghoul** is a Palestinian poet and academic. A graduate of Zagazig University, Egypt (1988), he has lectured in English literature at Al-Aqsa University, Gaza, since 1993. Ala'a's poetry often reflects on the trauma of war in Gaza, portraying the destruction of memory, identity, and human connection. His works emphasize resilience despite the devastation, finding hope and determination even amid despair. He has published numerous poetry collections, including: *All Seasons Are July* (1995), *Bahinbai: A Cave and a Lake* (1997), *Backstreet Story* (2005), *A Hundred Love Poems* (2015), *When the Gypsies Resemble You* (2015), *Autumn Pillows and the Color of Rain* (2015), *Casablanca Songs* (2016), *To Natasha, with All My Love* (2017), *Turquoise* (2017), *Cubes on a Slanted Edge* (2017), *Time Forgets and the City Is Empty* (2017), *Why Is It like This* (2017), *Neutral Expectations* (2018), *Lavender* (2018), *Bubbles of Sin and Love* (2018), *The Novel of Grass and Porcelain* (2020), *Artemis* (2020), *Silk Passion* (2021), and *Ziryab's Songs* (2021).

Dr. Kifah al-Ghusin is a Bedouin refugee from Beersheba who lives in the Gaza Strip. She is a writer and academic with a doctorate in media studies. She has published eight books, including her master's thesis, *The Reality of Literary Journalism in Palestinian Daily Newspapers* (2016); classical poetry collections

Tattoo on a Bedouin's Forehead (2000) and *I Knew God Through My Mother* (2017); a collection of Nabati poetry in Bedouin, *The Horse of Time* (2017); a collection of national and patriotic songs, *Pull Yourself Together, Country* (2017); a book of popular poetry, *May You Be Well* (2019); short stories for boys, *The Brave Boy* (2003); and a novel for boys, *Hankash: Diaries of the Pasture's Fantasy* (2023).

Born in Gaza, **Nema'a Hassan** is a feminist poet and fiction writer. She has authored two novels, *It Was Not Death* and *Letters Sent by a Woman.* In 2021, her translated poems on Gaza were published in the Harvard Divinity School's literary and arts journal, *Peripheries: A Journal of Word, Image, and Sound,* in a special folio guest-edited by Mosab Abu Toha and Tayseer Abu Odeh, alongside prominent Palestinian poets such as Hamid Ashour and Nasser Rabah.

Suleiman al-Hazeen's writing has been published in local and international newspapers, as well as on platforms such as the AlSharekh Archives, *Diwan al-Arab,* and the newspaper *Al-Hiayat al-Jadida,* among others. He is the winner of Best Prose Text Award in Gaza (2000) and was awarded the Dar Naji Nu'man Prize from Lebanon in 2008 for his collection of poetry *Lowering the Shadows,* which was published in multiple languages. He was awarded participation in the *Prince of Poets* competition (2008) and first prize at the Iraqi Poetry Festival in Belgrade (2012). His other poetry books include *Temptation in the Cave of Night* (2011), *Shores of Forgetfulness* (2015), and *The Cry of the Bitter Apple* (2021). He has been involved in the production of numerous theatrical verse plays in Palestine.

Othman Hussein, born in Rafah in the Gaza Strip in 1963, is the founder of the literary magazine *Ishtar* in the West Bank and Gaza. His seven poetry collections are *The Sailor Apologizes for Drowning*, *Who Will Decapitate the Sea?*, *You Are His*, *Things Left to the Blue*, *As if I Am Rolling the Galaxies*, *The Victim's Guard*, and, with Khaled Juma, *Rafah: An Alphabet of Distance and Memory*.

Hana al-Imsi is the author of the poetry works *The Lips of a Pen* (2016) and *The Neighing of Violins* (2018) and the theatrical operettas *Mimesis* and *The Cry of Jerusalem.* She regularly organizes and participates in poetry and literary gatherings in Gaza.

Hind Joudeh was born in 1983 in Gaza. She holds a bachelor's degree in educational technology from Al-Aqsa University, Gaza. Her publications include *Someone Always Leaves* (2014) and *No Sugar in the City* (2023). *A Finger That Could Survive* is forthcoming.

Author's note: My writing has been shaped by Palestine's occupation since 1948 and the siege on Gaza since 2006, the externally imposed conditions which have transformed this city into the largest open-air prison in the world. Deprivation and highly restricted choices have overshadowed my days for about eighteen years.

But writing remains the radiant fruit of my heart, even in electricity blackouts and with the constant droning of reconnaissance planes. My craft is a means of self-definition and understanding, reflecting the resilience and heartbreak of my people. Developed amid multiple wars on Gaza, my writing explores the tension between war's omnipresence and the yearning and continuous struggle for the semblance of an ordinary life.

Born in Rafah, Palestine, in 1965, **Khaled Juma** is a poet and children's author. He has published several collections of poetry, including *Strange Moon over the Flute Maker* (2022), *In War, Far from War* (2016), *Nothing Walks in Sleep* (2015), *So the Gypsy Doesn't Love You* (2012), *As the Horses Change* (2011), and *It's the Habit of Cities* (2009). He has published a collection of essays, *About My Martyred Friends* (2020), the short fiction *The White Horse's Suicide Night* (2018), the children's books *Corona Memoirs* (2021), *The Bull Who Stole the Kangaroo's Boots* (2019), *Memoirs of a Primary School Student* (2015), *The Rabbit Who Didn't Like His Name* (2012), *Three Legs* (2012), and *Plump and Sesame* (2010), and the young adult novels *The Tale Weaver* (2017) and *Maryam the Mute* (2016). There are translations of his work into languages such as Bulgarian, Danish, Dutch, English, French, German, Italian, Spanish, and Swedish. He is also the editor of various anthologies.

Dr. Nibal Khalil is an assistant professor of anthropology who completed her doctorate (2010) in social and cultural anthropology at Charles University in Prague. She has held various academic and research roles in Charles University's Faculty of Philosophy and has consulted widely on gender issues, women's empowerment, and youth leadership, and has worked with asylum services in Belgium. Since joining Al-Quds University in Palestine in 2014, Dr. Khalil has served as Dean of Scientific Research and taught in the Department of Applied Sociology. Currently, Dr. Khalil is an assistant professor and researcher at Birzeit University and teaches in the Graduate Department at the Arab American University in Palestine.

Her research explores Bedouin communities, violence against women, and higher education systems. She has presented at various international institutions and led workshops in Egypt, Lebanon, Palestine, Turkey, the United States, and across Europe.

Mohammad al-Khatib is editor in chief of the online creative magazine *Ibda'a.* His poetry collections include *The Victims' Tears* (2017) and *The Victims' Victory* (2019). His forthcoming books are *On the Bank of a Poem or . . .*, and *Engraved in Your Eyes, Oh Homeland.*

Author's note: In normal circumstances, it is almost impossible for a writer to craft a poem that embodies the dimensions of true poetry—voice, acute sensation, and originality—to convey the feelings of both writer and reader in a way that stirs the spirit and consciousness. Poetry is a miraculous labor of creation, like giving birth. And our poems are our daughters.

But what becomes of our poems in the face of despair, when hope is being destroyed along with the necessities of life? How can we write under the whistle of bullets and the roar of planes? They unload their deadly artillery, aiming also to annihilate the body of poems, to assassinate poetry.

Under such conditions, poets are endowed with a new imagination that unconsciously drives creativity and condenses expression. Poets must aim at density and brevity, and write with urgency and clarity, if they are to have any hope of delivering their message, uncertain whether it can be completed in ink and whether they will be obliged to append notes stained with blood.

The state of hope entwined with loss is cruel, unimaginable to people who haven't lived this reality—running from one crumbling wall to another, from one house to another, in a desperate bid to preserve the last text. Writing on a wall that is about to collapse is like sculpting with paper. But we let the text utter its agony and hope, embody the passion of the soul—its desire to finish the dream and manifest it.

Born in Gaza, Palestine, in 1959, **Yusra al-Khatib** holds a bachelor's degree in management and economics and a diploma in mathematics. She is the author of the novels *Stay Away* (2018) and *The City of Spiders* (2022); short story collections *And Sometimes the Sea Gets Thirsty* (2009), *Being with My Certainty* (2016), *Between Parentheses and a Star* (2018), a contribution to *Book of Gaza* (2014), and *A Clumsy Space* (forthcoming); and poetry collections *As If It Were a Homeland* (2013), *No Day of Judgment for You Now* (2020), *Seasons and More* (2021), and *Falling in Broad Daylight* and *The Water's Biography* (forthcoming). She is the winner of the fifth Creative Women Award for Short Stories. Her short stories and poems have been translated into English, French, and Kurdish.

Born in 1972 in Gaza, Palestine, **Maher al-Maqousi** holds a master's degree in civil engineering with a specialization in project management. His poetry collections are *Bleeding Stone* (1997), *To the End of the Wind* (2012), *They Were Crossing the Shadow* (2020), and *With Love I Came* (2023). The war has destroyed the press (Al-Kalima Publishing) preparing to release his fifth collection. Maher's poems have been featured in Arabic, European, and American newspapers, both in print and online. He was selected as one of the poets worldwide to write about the Palestinian cause for the anthology *Palestine: A Conscious Poetic Offering* (Inner Child Press, US, 2018).

Author's note: I ask myself if it is possible for those living outside of Gaza to truly imagine our extreme and bewildering grief, this repression, injustice, and the death. And the death. And the death and the death and the death. Martyrs are gone all at once. And the living—if it is right to call them *alive*—also depart daily in their own ways.

Everyone who lives in Gaza knows what it is to lose someone, again and again, every day, sometimes every hour. This murdering does not discriminate between people. Any minute you expect shrapnel to cut through your body or the bodies of your loved ones. Or perhaps the roof will collapse on you.

Shall I talk about what the war did to the body of the city? This city with whom we share a bond like the bond between a mother and her child? Every street is destroyed. The streets are fused to their houses. The bodies of fathers and mothers are welded to the bodies of their children. Everything is only the remains of everything—parents, children, streets, houses. Who is less fortunate?

Should I speak of our houses? Alongside them, we lost photographs of our parents and our childhoods, which we once showed our own children and were so eager to show our grandchildren too.

Shall I tell you about the houses that perished and their inhabitants who were killed, sometimes so quickly they didn't even notice it?

> I arrive at the house, but it has no door,
> no wood. In the thick smoke, it is timber.
> In the flames, are the children who played
> in the house's shade just yesterday.
> In their make-believe, they melted.
> They didn't run. You can see their smiles.
> Smiles also kill. They call to us wherever we go.

Shall I talk about my mother who lived through the first Nakba as a child when she couldn't possibly understand its meaning? When my mother left this world on January 1, 2024, she was still like a child. She was baffled by what she saw, she couldn't grasp its meaning. Just two days before her death, she asked me whether there are any cars. I asked, *For what?* She answered in a belligerent tone, *To go back to our home.*

Shall I talk about the children of Gaza? The children did not know what war is, what massacre is. They were just like the other children of this world who jump with joy for the sake of a doll. Today they know why their names are being written along their arms.

Shall I speak of the sand of Gaza? It is not sand. It is remains. Everyone who walks across it should walk lightly, gently, and should recite whatever prayer or scripture they can.

Shall I speak of our audience who grows accustomed to these scenes until our deaths have become mundane to them? This is one of our biggest catastrophes—other people see our deaths as routine.

I still remember Darwish saying *We love life as much as we can.* Yes, we love life. Its value for us is equal to the value it has for all others, and no sacrifice has any value without it.

Dr. Ala'a al-Qatrawi, born in 1990, holds a PhD in Arabic literature and criticism (2022); her dissertation, *Mirrors in the Poetry of Adonis: A Semiotic Study*, is the first extensive theoretical application of semiotics to the work of the Syrian poet. She is a former radio presenter, having hosted the poetry programs *On the Euphrates of Poetry* (2013) and *The Talk of the Soul* (2010).

Her own poetry has won several awards, including the Abdulaziz al-Babtain Prize for Best Poetry Collection by a Young Poet (2022). She was a semifinalist in the live-broadcast rounds of *Prince of Poets* (season 7, 2017) and received first place in the See You Soon competition for the poem "Finer than the Ney" (2015). In 2013, she won first place for her poem "A Slender Moon" in the Rocks from the Sky competition. In 2012, she won first place in the Revolution of Ink competition. Her short stories have also won awards, most recently first place in the Those Stories international competition.

Ala'a writes lyrics for popular songs, including "You Promised Me," performed by Palestinian artist Mais Shalash, and has authored and staged several poetry operettas, such as *Freedom Sings* (2013) and *Thawer* (2012). She participated in writing reflections on Palestinian prisoners' photos for the *Souls, Not Pictures* exhibition (2013, 2014).

Maryam Qawwash is a Palestinian poet, born in 1988 in the Al-Nuseirat Refugee Camp in Gaza. She is a doctoral candidate in the philosophy of literature at Tanta University, Egypt. Her poetry collections are *Seven Years of Famine* (2017), *As the Quail Walks* (2019), *Letters to the Orange* (2021), *Belonging to the Daylight* (2023), and *Then It Blossoms Again* (2023). She has received numerous poetry prizes, including the Poetry Prize in the Faculty of Arts of the Islamic University (2013), the ninth Palestine International Poetry Prize for *Letters to the Orange,* the Palestine State Encouragement Prize for Young Creators for *As the Quail Walks,* the Mediterranean Poetry Prize (2022), the second Antoun Saadeh Poetry Prize for *Belonging to the Daylight,* and the ninth Al Burda Award for Poetry (second prize, 2023).

Born in Gaza in 1963, **Nasser Rabah** is a celebrated Palestinian poet who has been translated into English, Hebrew, and French. He received his bachelor's degree in agricultural science from Ain Shams University in Egypt. He has published a novel, *About an Hour Ago* (2018), and several collections of poetry, including *Eulogy for the Robin* (2020), *Water Thirsty for Water* (2016), *Passersby with Invisible Clothing* (2013), and *Running After Dead Gazelles* (2003). English translations of his poetry appear in the *Los Angeles Review of Books, The New Yorker, The Paris Review,* and *Poetry,* among other magazines. A translated collection of his poems, *Gaza: The Poem Said Its Piece* (2025), is in the City Lights Pocket Poets Series.

Author's note: I wrestle anxiously with the act of writing amid war. What does writing mean when our lives hang in the balance—there seems to be no room for reflection, for poetry, for an audience. Writing is distilled into one genre: bearing witness. I must chronicle the daily catastrophes in Gaza, capture their rhythms, confine them to language. But a relentless question haunts me: how does one stubbornly pursue poetry's prey, and hold it before the face of this ghastly bloodshed, this rubble, the dead, these ruins of our lives, when we are also being hunted—when our flesh, our souls are being torn apart?

But writing has become an inescapable duty in these terrifying times, like praying over a martyr, bidding farewell to a friend, or maneuvering through the omnipresence of death, for writing is also a relentless struggle, pushing a boulder of resilience up the steep mountain of tragedy. Writing is an art of survival. It is also a labor of love, and I cherish it. Writers have a duty to use their art to comfort the bereaved and give them hope, to affirm our nationhood, our morality, and assure Palestinians that we endure—we defy erasure.

Writing is a form of resistance, a way to deny our tormentors the satisfaction of triumph. So, we keep writing. We owe it to our martyrs and to the orphaned children. We owe it to history, to justice, and to the truth that does not perish.

Shuja'a al-Safadi is a Palestinian poet and writer from Gaza. He has a master's degree in international economic relations from Kharkiv National University and several published works: *I Lean on a Stone* (2005), *The Remnants of the Pain* (2006), *Travel Through the Void* (2009), *An Act of Deception* (2009), *Wheat Flees to the Grindstone* (2012), *A Dove Without a Song* (2019), and *A Dream's Lapse* (2020).

Khaled Shaheen was born in 1968. His poetry publications include *I Am Not Khaled* (2016) and *Echo of the Whip* (2018). His forthcoming books are *Empty of Them, Full of You* and *To Zakaria Mohammed.*

Jabir Sha'ith has published several collections of poetry: *A Thousand B's* (2003), *White Sins* (2008), *As If I Am* (2010), *Stray Biography* (2012), *The First She-Wolf on the Road* (2023), *Beyond the Metaphor* (2024), and *The Seventh Balcony of the House* (forthcoming).

Born in 1997, **Hashem Shalola** resides in Gaza. He holds a bachelor's degree in Arabic language from Al-Aqsa University and writes poetry, fiction, and literary criticism. He has published many collections of poetry, including *Telegrams to a Broken Fax Machine, The Wolf Will Devour the Attentive, What If They Knew We Are Strangers?,* and *Who Will Convince the Sea That This Sadness Is Enough?* He contributed to the 2022 anthology *Gaza, terra da poesia.*

Hala al-Shrouf, born in Libya in 1978, is the director of publications at the Palestinian Museum in the West Bank. Hala is a poet, translator, and editor, specializing in editing children's and young adult literature and writing for museums, and she is the mother of three children: Khaled, Ammar, and Dalia. She has translated a novel by Suad Amiry and Hala Sakakini's memoir *Me and Jerusalem.* She has published two collections of poetry: *I Will Follow Clouds* (2005) and *I Didn't Cut the River* (2014).

Born in Gaza in 1982, **Yasir al-Waqqad** holds a bachelor's degree in geography and works as an educator, organizing numerous poetry evenings and critical seminars in the Gaza Strip. Yasir has won several prestigious awards, including the Mediterranean Poetry Prize in 2022. In 2023, he published four poetry collections: *A Cinematic Hook, A Peripatetic in the Gardens of Destiny, The Celestial Identity,* and *Barefoot on the Sands of the Moon.* Previous collections include *Songs of the Waterwheel, The Phoenix Camps, Hosted by September, Lemon Poems, The Minarets of the Cactus,* and *The Flowers of the Blind.*

Author's note: Writing in the besieged city of Gaza is an aesthetic and existential ordeal. The rubble, the corpses. The dying is ongoing and daily. The ink of language can transform into blood and oil, coated in dust and curses. This is what I have undergone since the outbreak of war—lava fell in an inferno around my rural house in Gaza. By the end of October 2023, I was forced to leave it. I was displaced from one shelter to another, wandering aimlessly, until I settled temporarily in a refugee camp whose tents and fragile wishes are planted in our sand.

Ghassan Zaqtan, born in Beit Jala, near Bethlehem, is a prolific poet and writer with over ten poetry collections and several works of prose, including a novel and a play. His collection *Like a Straw Bird It Follows Me,* translated by Fady Joudah for Yale University Press, was awarded the Griffin Poetry Prize in 2013. *The Silence That Remains* was published in 2017 by Copper Canyon Press. These translations were reprinted by Smokestack Books in London and Seagull Books in India. He was shortlisted for the Neustadt International Prize for Literature (perceived as the American Nobel Prize) in 2014 and again in 2016. His name appeared for the first time in 2013 among the favorites to win the Nobel Prize. He was a recipient of the Mahmoud Darwish Excellence Award for poetry in 2016 and won the first Anwar Salman Award in 2019. He writes two weekly columns for the Palestinian newspaper *Al-Ayyam* and the Beirut-based publication *Al-Nahar.* Having lived in Jordan, Syria, Lebanon, and Tunisia, Ghassan currently resides in Ramallah, Palestine. Photo by Dirk Skiba.

Born in 1987, **Fida'a Zayed** is a writer and teacher who lives in the Gaza Strip. She holds a bachelor's degree in Arabic language and teaching methodology and a diploma in Arabic literature and criticism. She organizes educational, literary, and cultural events in Gaza.

About the Translators and Editors

Tayseer Abu Odeh is a Palestinian-Jordanian writer and scholar. He is an associate professor of comparative literature in Jordan. His book of creative nonfiction, *The Consolations of Exile,* was published in Beirut in 2019. His translation of Samuel Moyn's *Liberalism Against Itself: Cold War Intellectuals and the Making of Our Times* is forthcoming from the Arab Network Press in October 2025. His poems and articles appear in *Michigan Quarterly Review, Peripheries, Journal of Postcolonial Writing, Middle Eastern Literatures, The Journal of Holy Land and Palestine Studies, The Harvard Crimson,* and elsewhere.

Sherah Bloor is a South African poet and scholar. Her first collection, *The Gathering,* is forthcoming from Omnidawn in fall 2026. She is currently working on a second book, tentatively titled *Archives of the Free World.* Sherah is also completing a doctorate in philosophy of religion on the medical history of the imagination at Harvard University, where she is the editor-in-chief of the literary and arts journal *Peripheries: A Journal of Word, Image, and Sound* (Harvard University Press). Her poems have appeared in *Best New Poets 2024, Chicago Review, Colorado Review, Conjunctions, Dialogist, Lana Turner,* and *Paperbark,* among other magazines. Photo by Ashley Borders Zigman.

Copper Canyon Press is deeply grateful to the following individuals and organizations whose philanthropic vision and love of poetry made *You Must Live* possible.

Anonymous

Daniel Cogan

Geralyn White Dreyfous

Firehouse Fund

Jorie Graham

Rashid and Mona Khalidi

The Madrona Fund

The Maude Giving Fund

V (formerly Eve Ensler)

Ocean Vuong

Davis and Betsy Weinstock

Jamie Wolf

POETS FOR POETRY

Copper Canyon Press poets are at the center of all our efforts as a nonprofit publisher. Poets create the art of our books, and they read and teach the books we publish. Many are also generous donors who believe in financially supporting the vibrant poetry community of Copper Canyon Press. For decades, our poets have quietly donated their royalties, have contributed their time to our fundraising campaigns, and have made personal donations in support of emerging and established poets. Their generosity has encouraged the innovative risk-taking that sustains and furthers the art form.

The donor-poets who have contributed to the Press since 2023 include:

Jonathan Aaron
Pamela Alexander
Kazim Ali
Ellen Bass
Erin Belieu
Mark Bibbins
Linda Bierds
Sherwin Bitsui
Jaswinder Bolina
Marianne Boruch
Laure-Anne Bosselaar
Cyrus Cassells
Peter Cole and Adina Hoffman
Elizabeth J. Coleman
Shangyang Fang
John Freeman
Forrest Gander
Jenny George
Dan Gerber
Jorie Graham
Roger Greenwald
Robert and Carolyn Hedin
Bob Hicok
Ha Jin
The estate of Jaan Kaplinski
Laura Kasischke
Jennifer L. Knox
Ted Kooser
Stephen Kuusisto
Deborah Landau
Sung-Il Lee
Ben Lerner
Dana Levin
Maurice Manning
Heather McHugh
Jane Miller
Roger Mitchell
Lisa Olstein
Gregory Orr
Eric Pankey
Kevin Prufer
Alicia Rabins
Dean Rader
Paisley Rekdal
James Richardson
Alberto Ríos
David Romtvedt
Sarah Ruhl
Kelli Russell Agodon
Natalie Shapero
Arthur Sze
Yuki Tanaka
Elaine Terranova
Chase Twichell
Ocean Vuong
Connie Wanek
Emily Warn

Poetry is vital to language and living. Since 1972, Copper Canyon Press has published extraordinary poetry from around the world to engage the imaginations and intellects of readers, writers, booksellers, librarians, teachers, students, and donors.

We are grateful for the major support provided by:

academy of american poets

ARTSFUND

THE PAUL G. ALLEN FAMILY FOUNDATION

TO LEARN MORE ABOUT UNDERWRITING
COPPER CANYON PRESS TITLES,
PLEASE CALL 360-385-4925 EXT. 105

WE ARE GRATEFUL FOR THE MAJOR SUPPORT PROVIDED BY:

Anonymous
Jill Baker and Jeffrey Bishop
Mona Baroudi and Patrick Whitgrove
Lisha Bian
Rick Shinsui Bowles
John Branch
Diane and Dorothy Brooks Foundation
Diana Broze
John R. Cahill
Sarah J. Cavanaugh
Keith Cowan and Linda Walsh
Peter Currie
Geralyn White Dreyfous
The Evans Family
Mimi Gardner Gates
Claire Gribbin
Gull Industries Inc. on behalf of William True
Carolyn and Robert Hedin
David and Jane Hibbard
Bruce S. Kahn
Phil Kovacevich and Eric Wechsler
Eric La Brecque
Maureen Lee and Mark Busto
Ellie Mathews and Carl Youngmann as The North Press
Kathryn O'Driscoll
Petunia Charitable Fund and advisor Elizabeth Hebert
Suzanne Rapp and Mark Hamilton
Adam and Lynn Rauch
Emily and Dan Raymond
Joseph C. Roberts
Cynthia Sears
Kim and Jeff Seely
Tree Swenson
Julia Sze
Donna Wolf
Jamie Wolf
Barbara and Charles Wright
In honor of C.D. Wright from Forrest Gander
Caleb Young as C. Young Creative
The dedicated interns and faithful volunteers of Copper Canyon Press

The pressmark for Copper Canyon Press
suggests entrance, connection, and interaction
while holding at its center
an attentive, dynamic space for poetry.

English text in this book is set in Didot LT Pro.
The Arabic text is set in Adobe Arabic.
Book design and composition by E. Rowan Mena.
Printed in Canada on archival-quality paper.